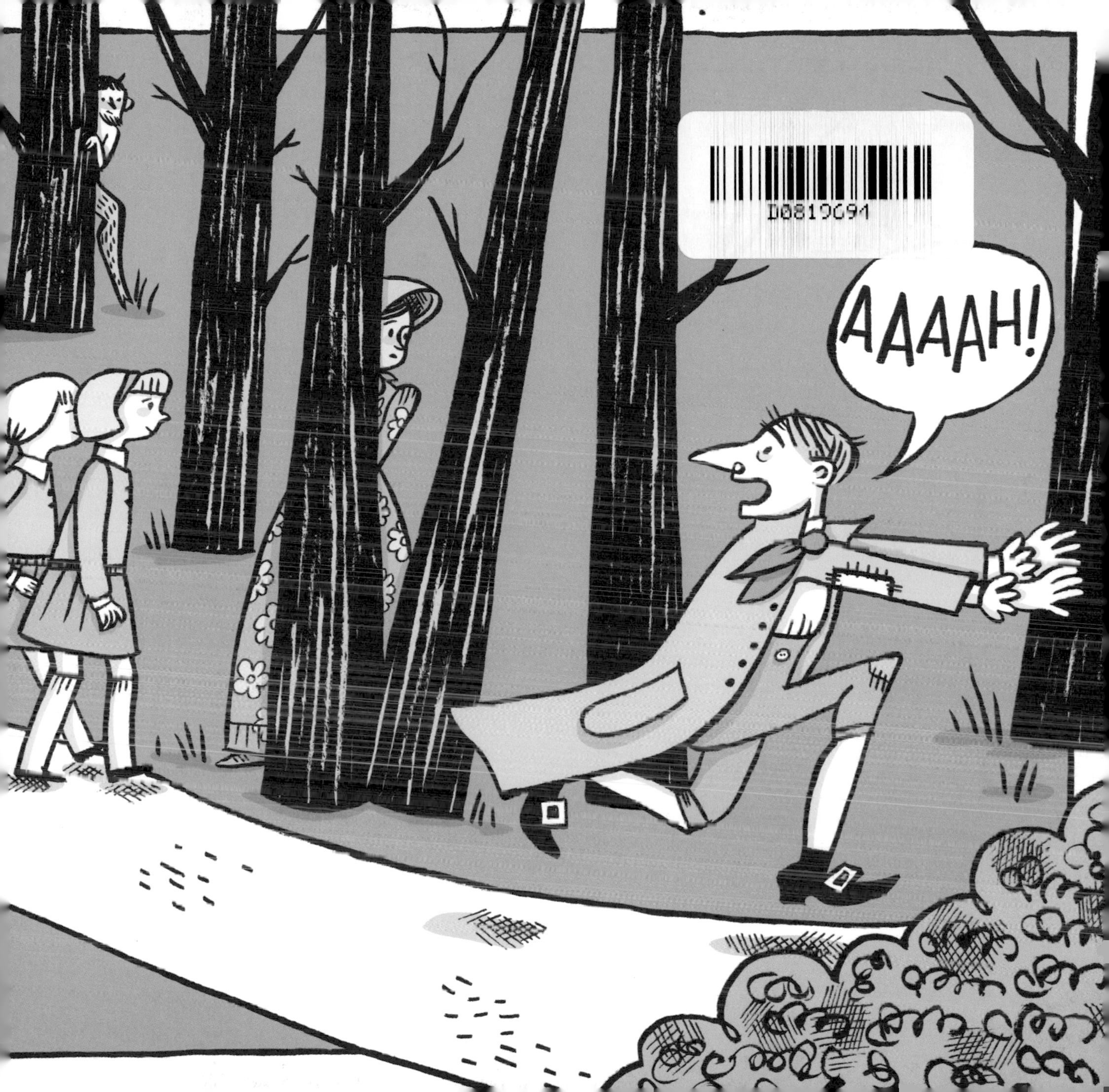
AAAAH!

LONG STORY SHORT

100 CLASSIC BOOKS in 3 PANELS

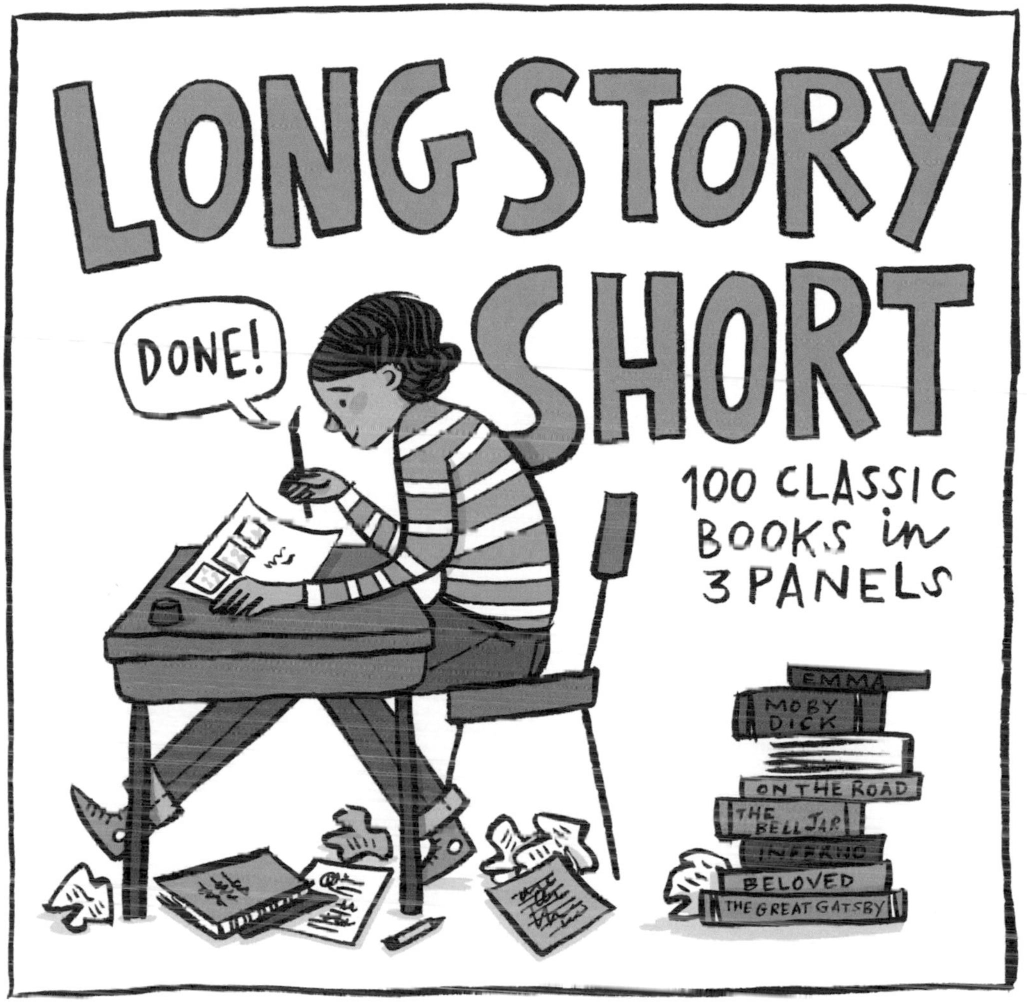
LONG STORY SHORT
DONE!
100 CLASSIC BOOKS in 3 PANELS
EMMA
MOBY DICK
ON THE ROAD
THE BELL JAR
INFERNO
BELOVED
THE GREAT GATSBY

A COMIC STRIP COLLECTION by LISA BROWN

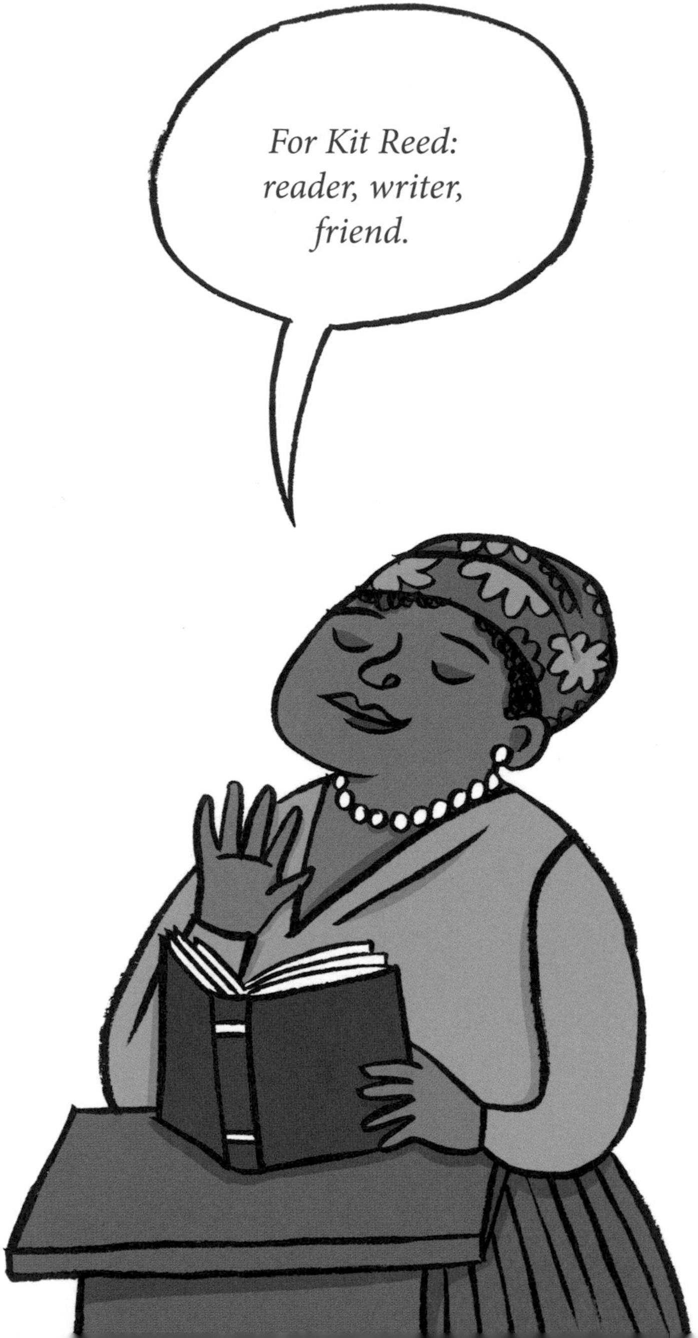
For Kit Reed: reader, writer, friend.

Published by Algonquin Books of Chapel Hill
Post Office Box 2225, Chapel Hill, North Carolina 27515-2225

a division of Workman Publishing
225 Varick Street, New York, New York 10014

Printed in Malaysia.
Published simultaneously in Canada by
Thomas Allen & Son Limited.
Design by Lisa Brown.

10 9 8 7 6 5 4 3 2 1
First Edition

Library of Congress Cataloging-in-Publication Data
Names: Brown, Lisa, 1972- author.
Title: Long story short : 100 classic books in 3 panels ;
a comic strip collection / by Lisa Brown.
Description: Chapel Hill : Algonquin Books of Chapel Hill, 2020. | Includes index. |
Summary: "One hundred pithy and skewering three-panel literary summaries, from curriculum classics like Don Quixote, Lord of the Flies, and Jane Eyre to modern favorites like Beloved, The Brief Wondrous Life of Oscar Wao, and Atonement, conveniently organized by subjects including 'Love,' 'Sex,' 'Death,' and 'Female Trouble.' "–Provided by publisher.
Identifiers: LCCN 2019027459 | ISBN 9781616205034 (hardcover) |
ISBN 9781643750613 (ebook)
Subjects: LCGFT: Graphic novels.
Classification: LCC PN6727.B75765 L66 2020 | DDC 741.5/973–dc23
LC record available at https://lccn.loc.gov/2019027459

Acknowledgment is made to the following publications in which many of these cartoons originally appeared, some in slightly different form: the *San Francisco Chronicle*; the *New York Times*; *Half-Minute Horrors*, edited by Susan Rich; *The Graphic Canon, Volume 3*, edited by Russ Kick; and *Depressed. Repressed. Obsessed* by Lisa Brown, published in conjunction with California Bookstore Day.

The art in this book was created with india ink on paper and colored digitally.

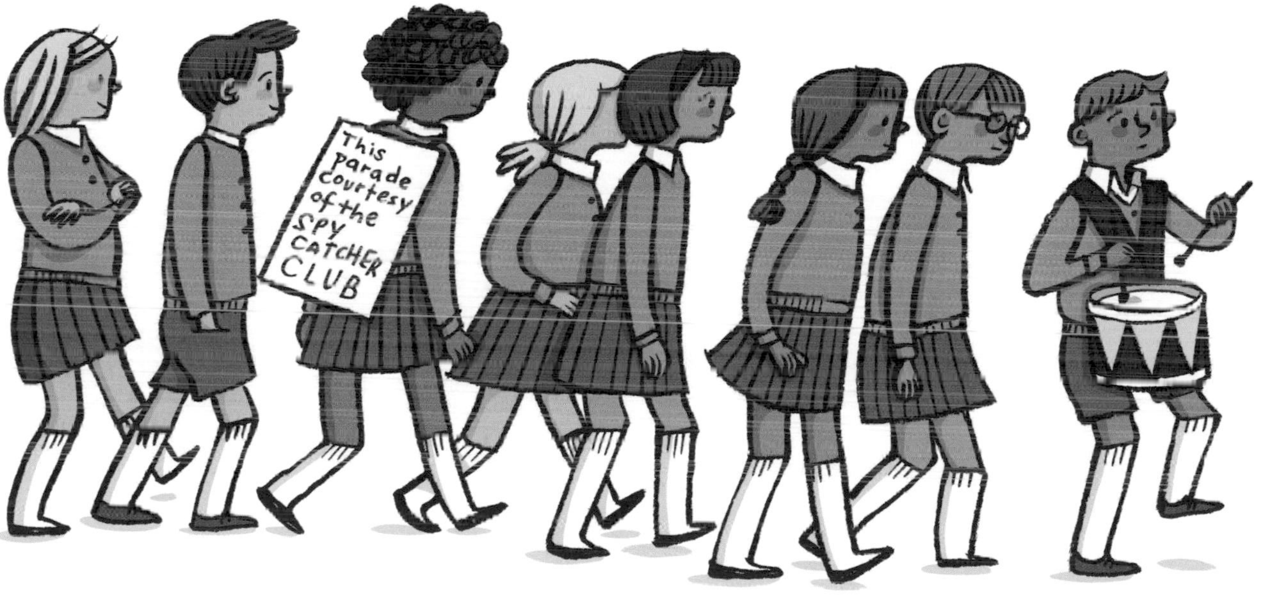
This parade courtesy of the SPY CATCHER CLUB

CONTENTS

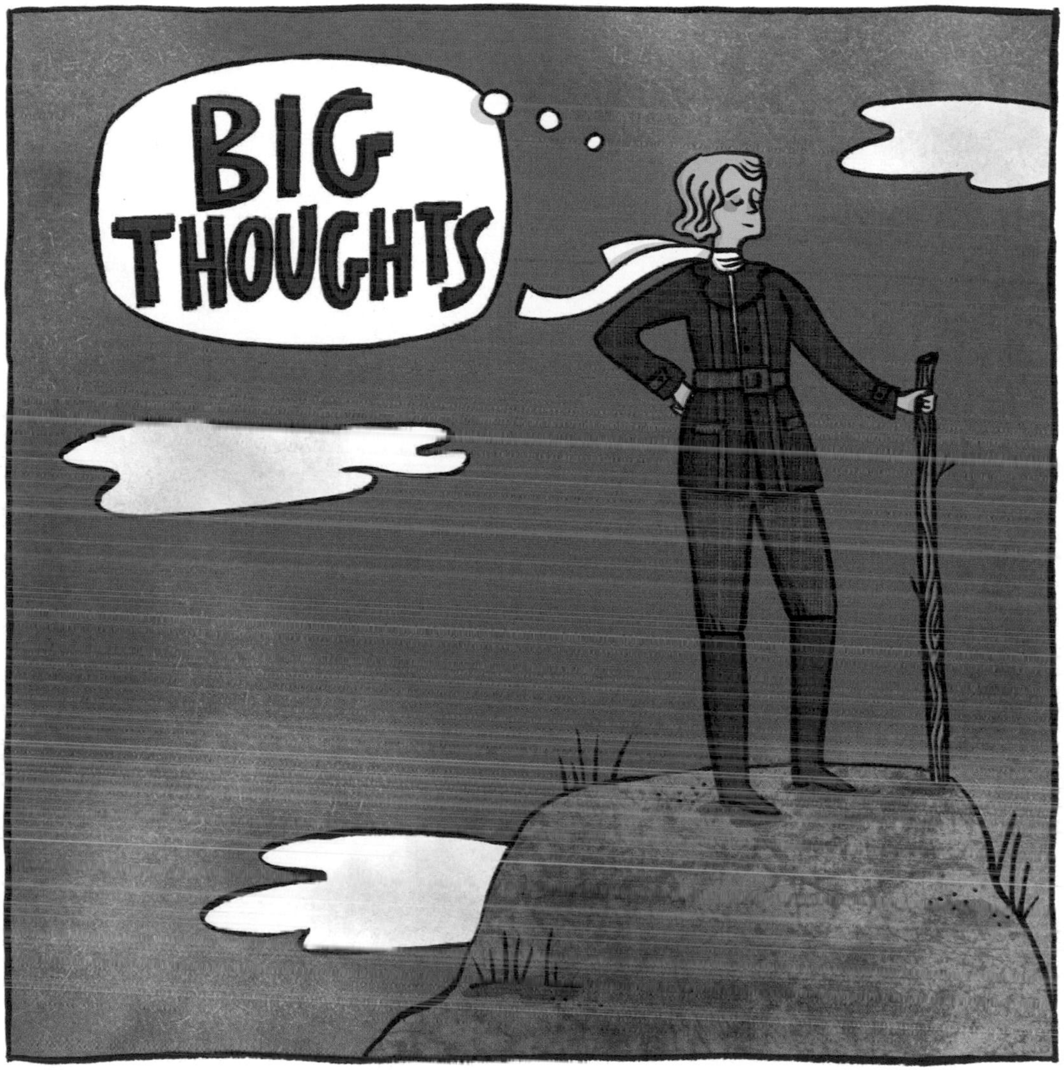
BIG THOUGHTS

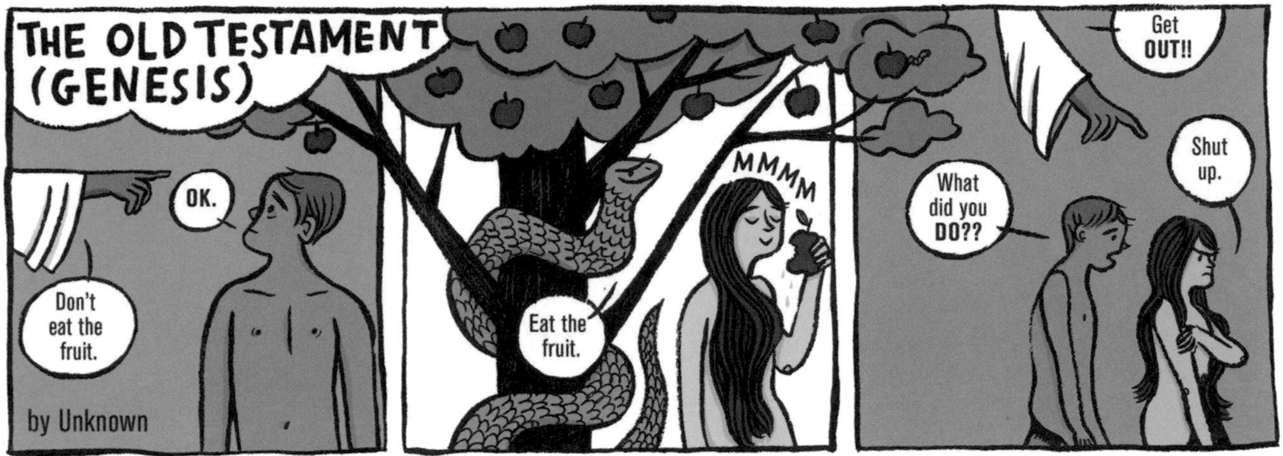
THE OLD TESTAMENT (GENESIS)
by Unknown
Don't eat the fruit.
OK.
Eat the fruit.
MMMM
Get OUT!!
What did you DO??
Shut up.

SEE "SEX"

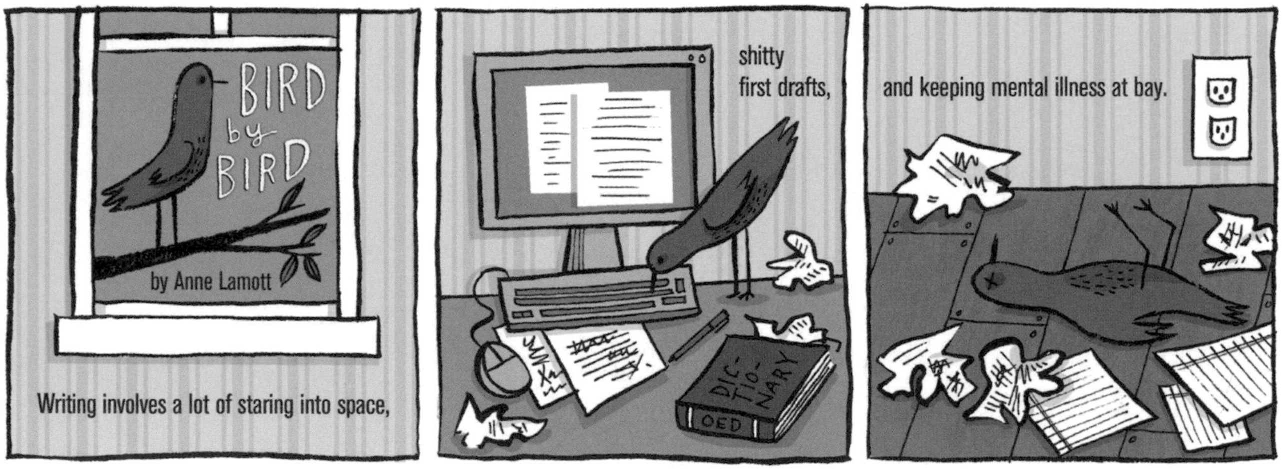
BIRD by BIRD
by Anne Lamott
Writing involves a lot of staring into space,
shitty first drafts,
DIC-TIO-NARY
OED
and keeping mental illness at bay.

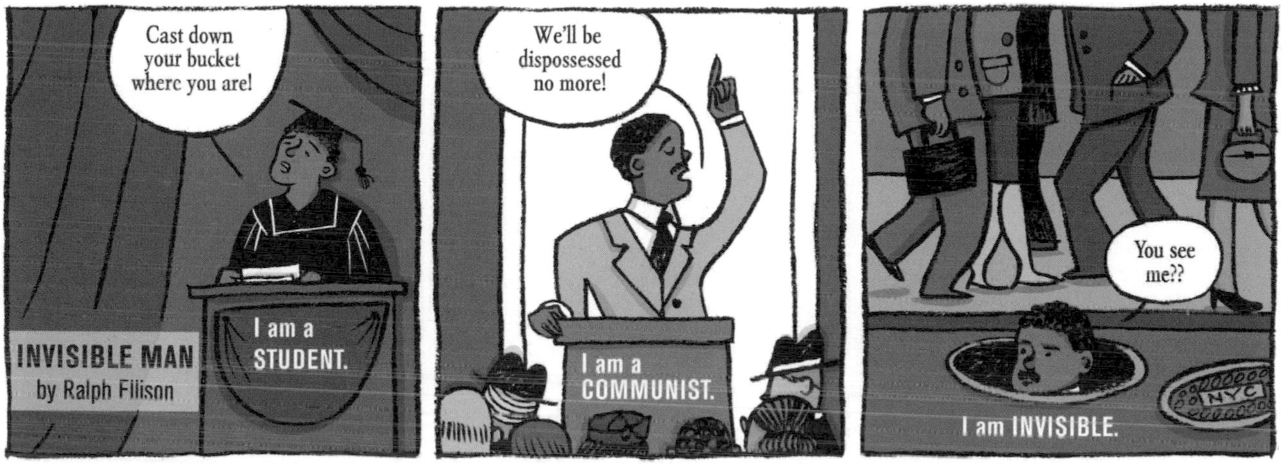
Cast down your bucket where you are!
INVISIBLE MAN
by Ralph Ellison
I am a STUDENT.
We'll be dispossessed no more!
I am a COMMUNIST.
You see me??
NYC
I am INVISIBLE.

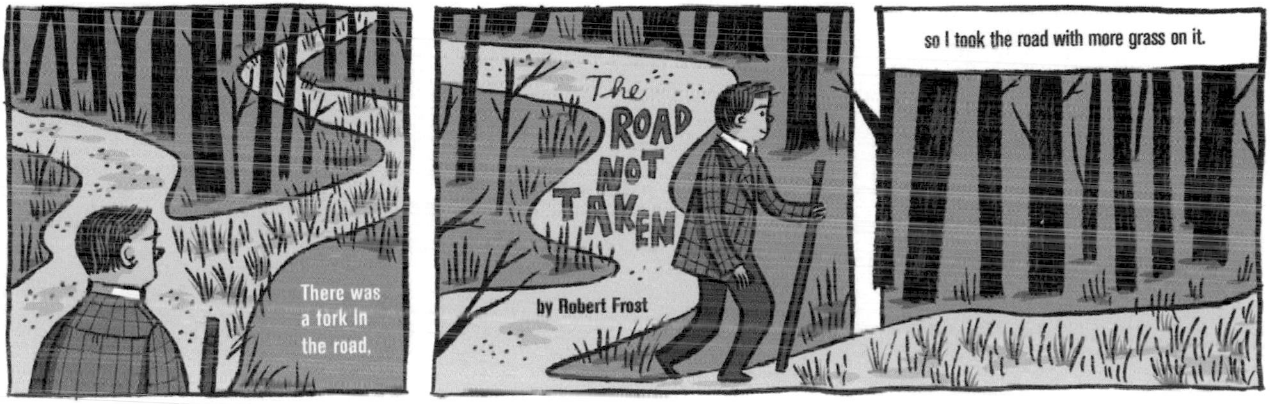
There was a fork in the road,
The ROAD NOT TAKEN
by Robert Frost
so I took the road with more grass on it.

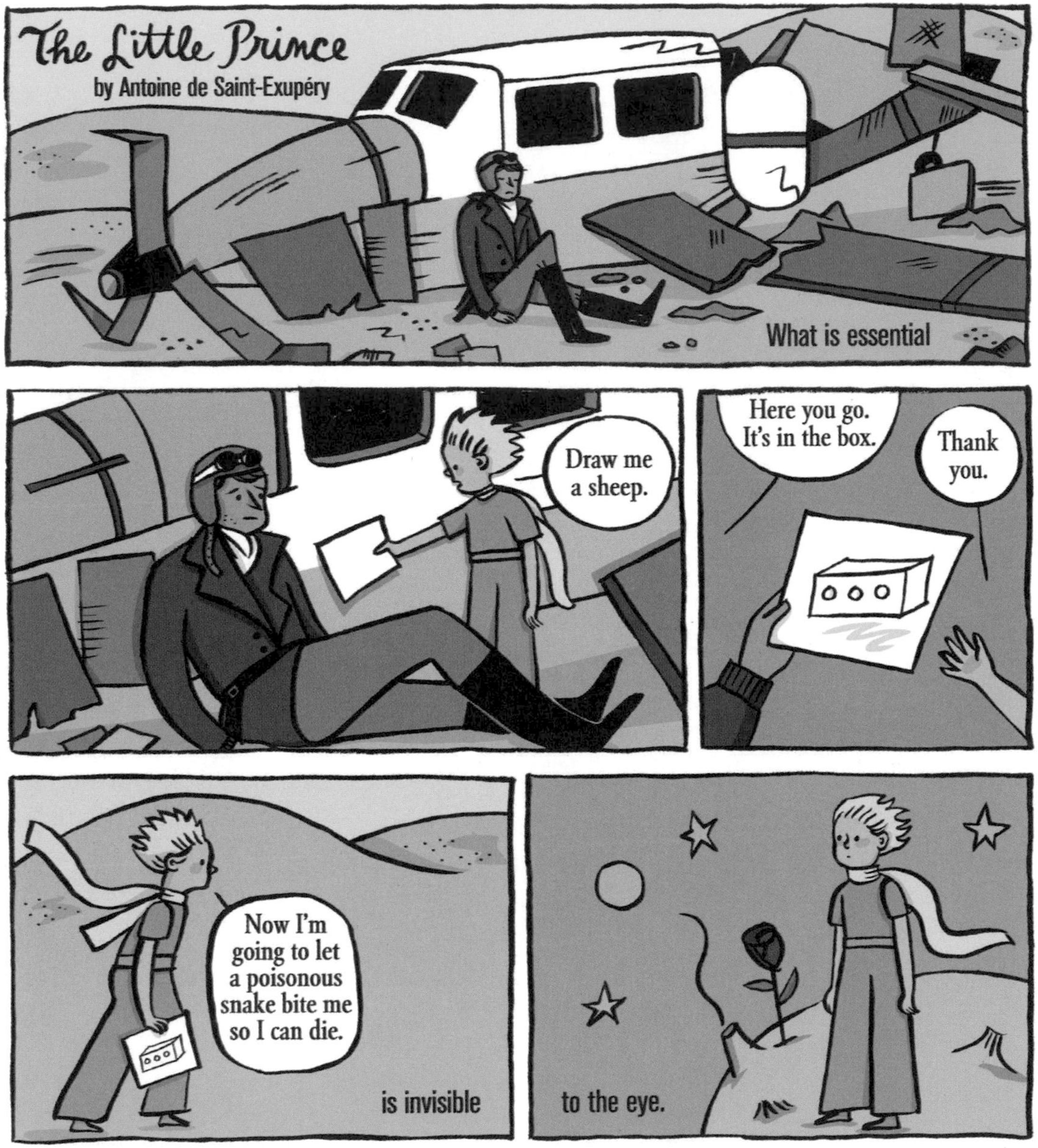
The Little Prince
by Antoine de Saint-Exupéry
What is essential
Draw me a sheep.
Here you go. It's in the box.
Thank you.
Now I'm going to let a poisonous snake bite me so I can die.
is invisible
to the eye.

SEE "EPIC"

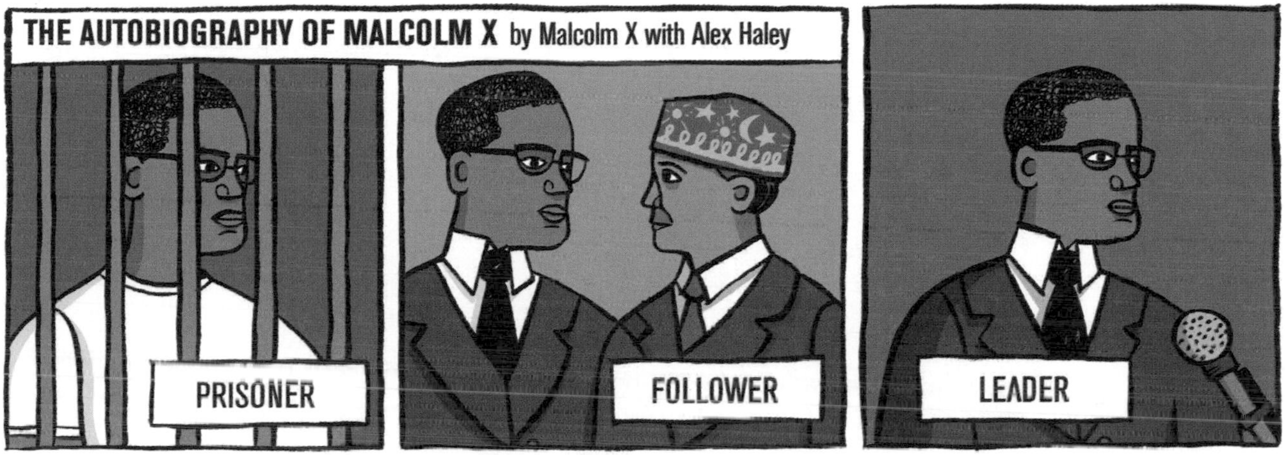
THE AUTOBIOGRAPHY OF MALCOLM X by Malcolm X with Alex Haley
PRISONER
FOLLOWER
LEADER

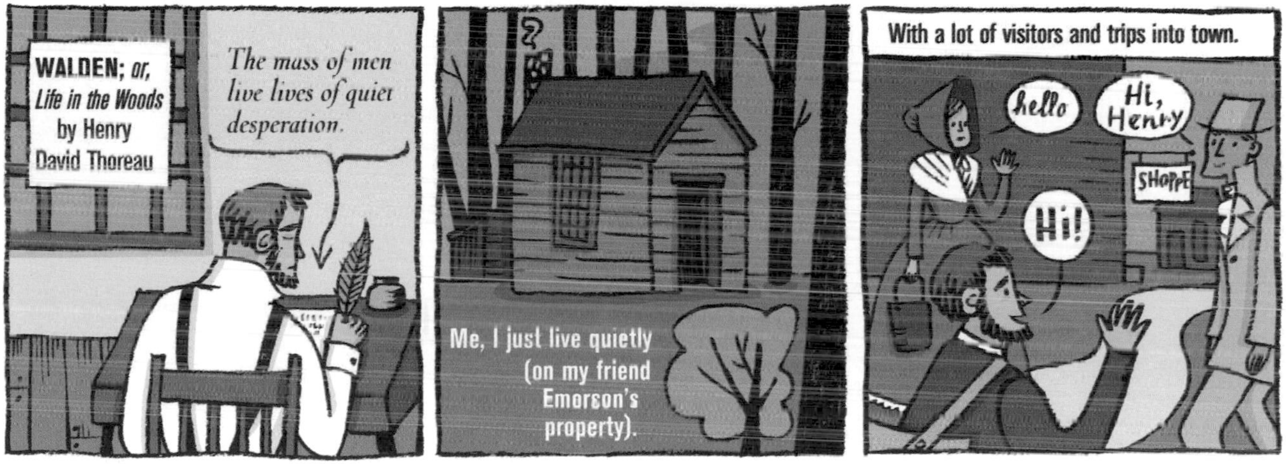
WALDEN; or, Life in the Woods by Henry David Thoreau
The mass of men live lives of quiet desperation.
Me, I just live quietly (on my friend Emerson's property).
With a lot of visitors and trips into town.
hello
Hi, Henry
SHOPPE
Hi!

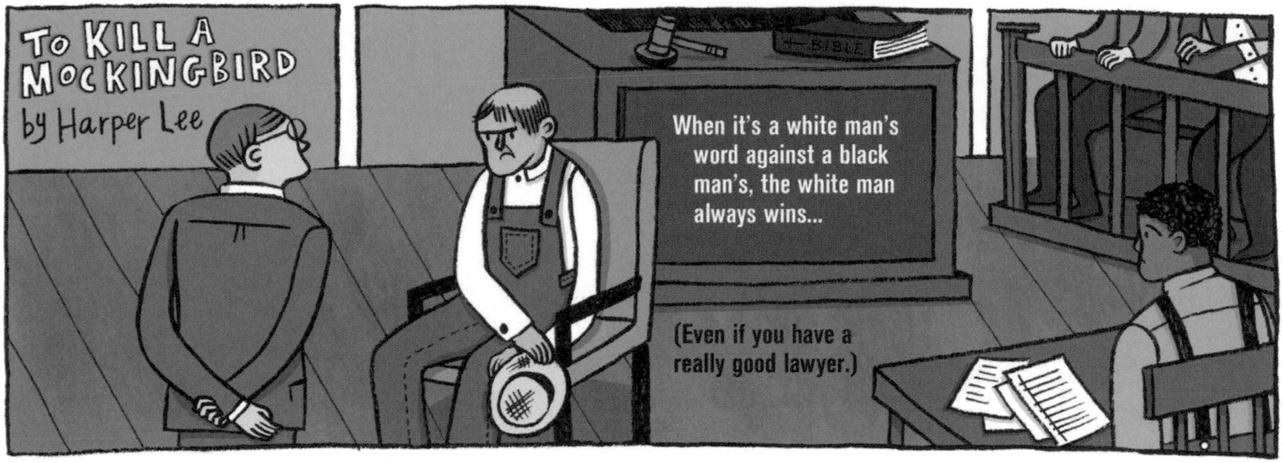
To KILL A MOCKINGBIRD
by Harper Lee
BIBLE
When it's a white man's word against a black man's, the white man always wins...
(Even if you have a really good lawyer.)

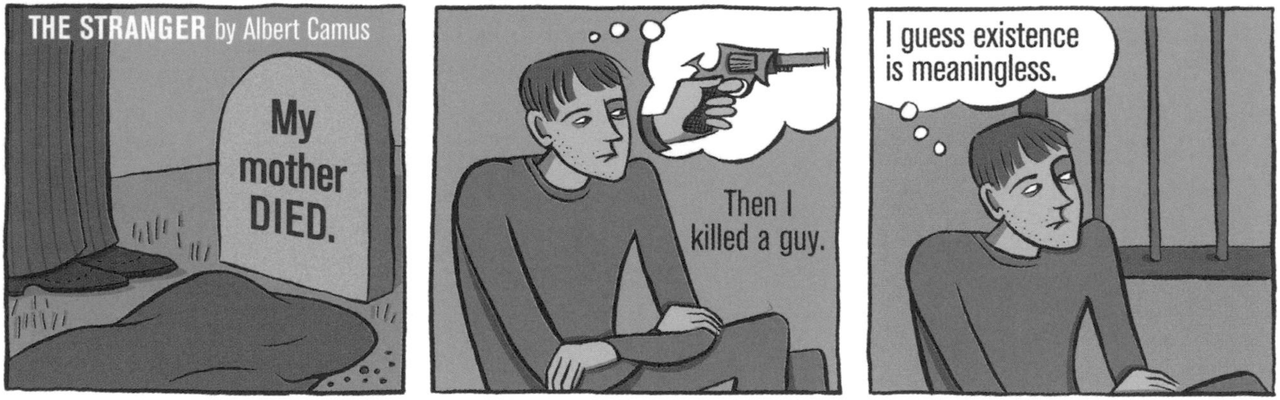
THE STRANGER by Albert Camus
My mother DIED.
Then I killed a guy.
I guess existence is meaningless.

SEE "DEATH"

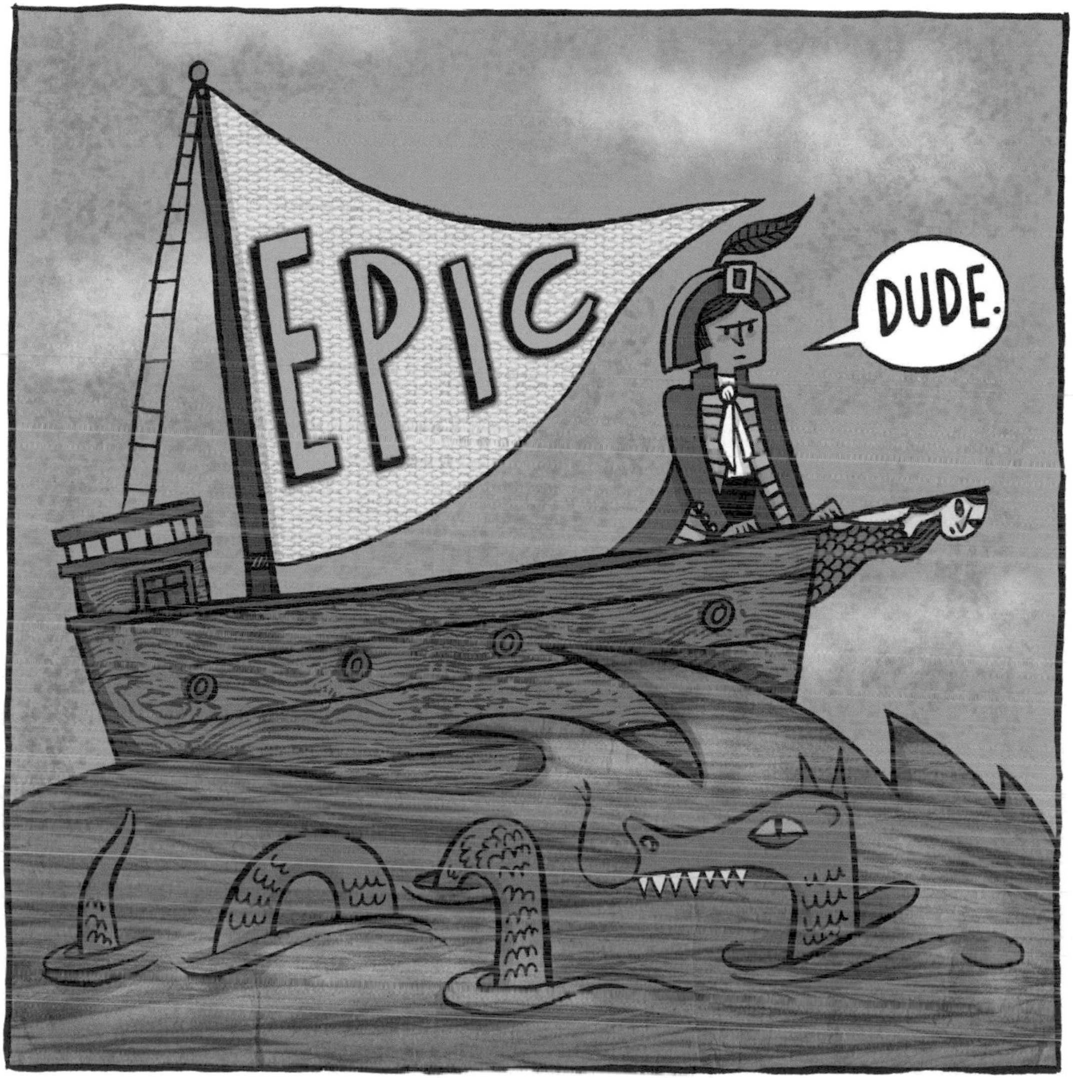
EPIC
DUDE.

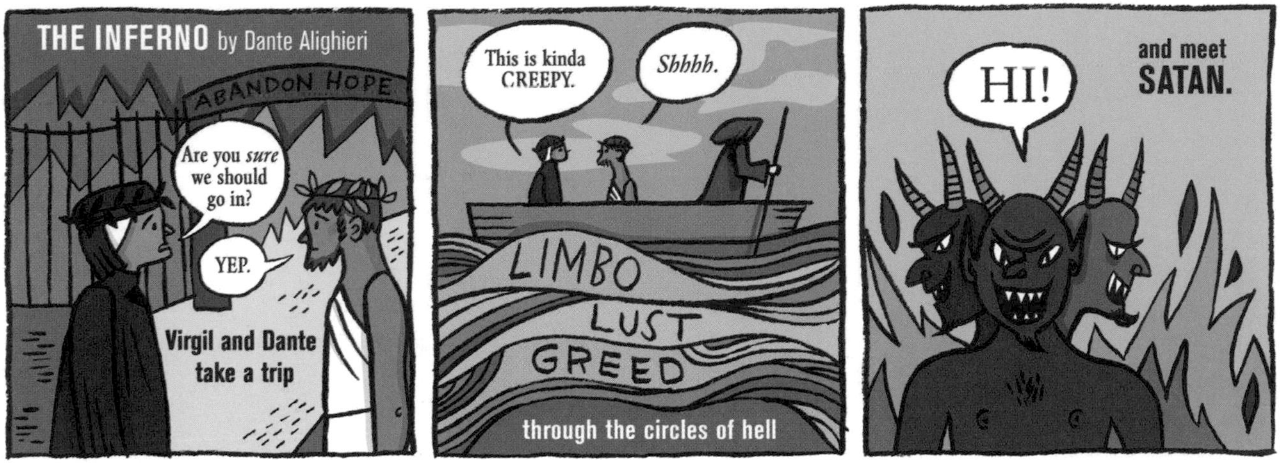
THE INFERNO by Dante Alighieri
ABANDON HOPE
Are you *sure* we should go in?
YEP.
Virgil and Dante take a trip
This is kinda CREEPY.
Shhhh.
LIMBO
LUST
GREED
through the circles of hell
HI!
and meet SATAN.

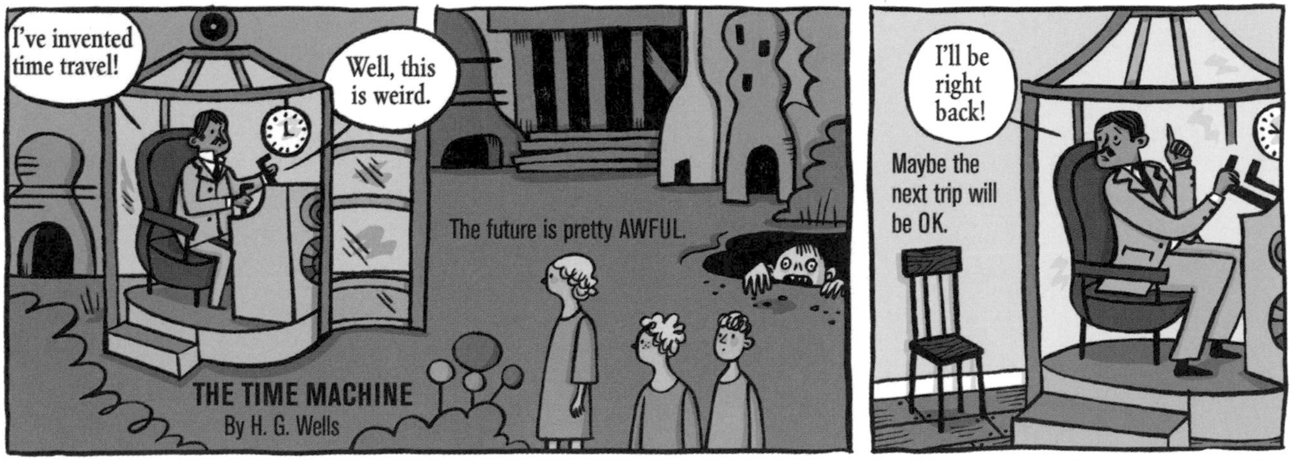
I've invented time travel!
Well, this is weird.
The future is pretty AWFUL.
THE TIME MACHINE
By H. G. Wells
I'll be right back!
Maybe the next trip will be OK.

SEE "CREATURES"

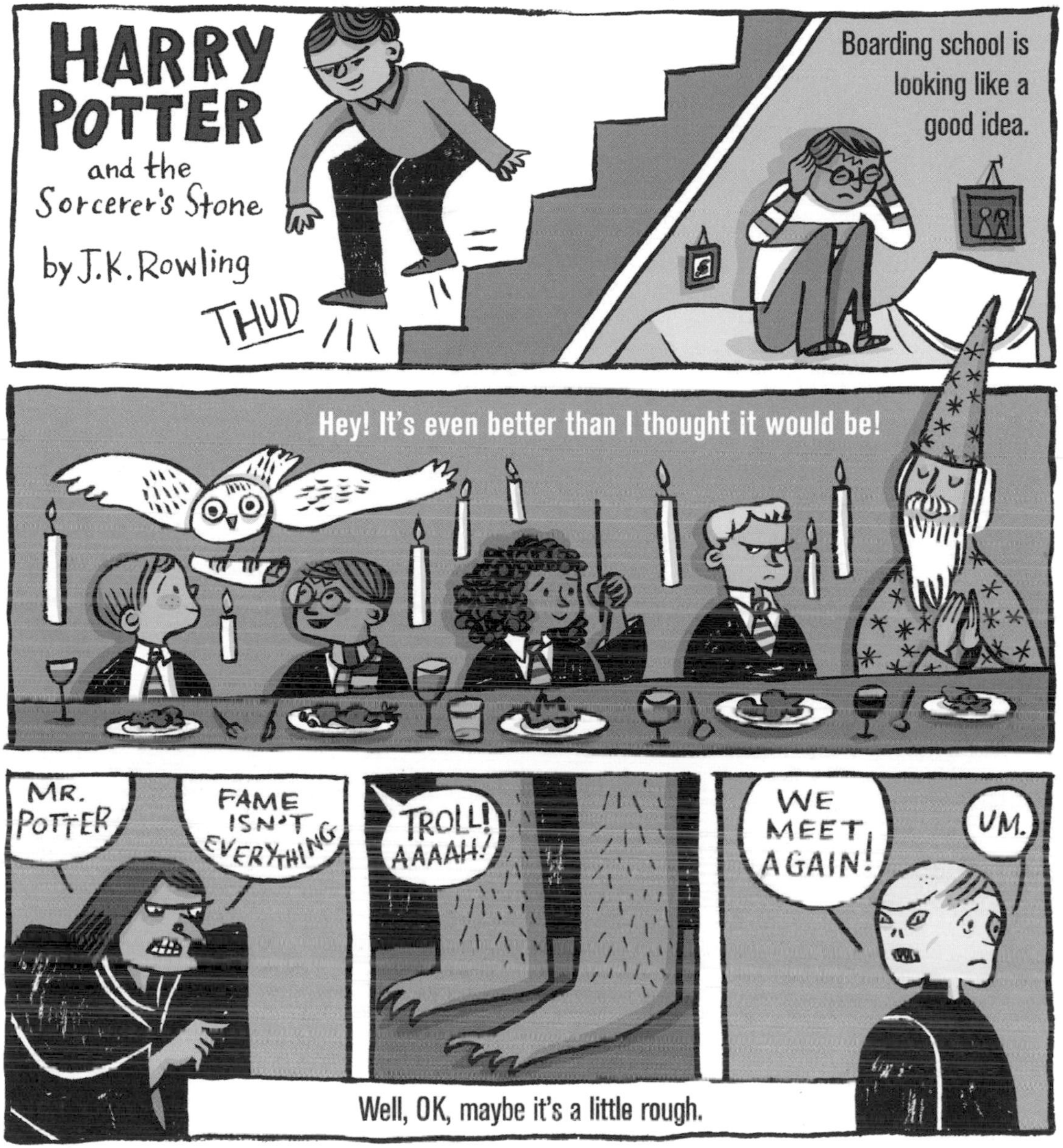
HARRY POTTER
and the Sorcerer's Stone
by J.K. Rowling
THUD
Boarding school is looking like a good idea.
Hey! It's even better than I thought it would be!
MR. POTTER
FAME ISN'T EVERYTHING
TROLL! AAAAH!
WE MEET AGAIN!
UM.
Well, OK, maybe it's a little rough.

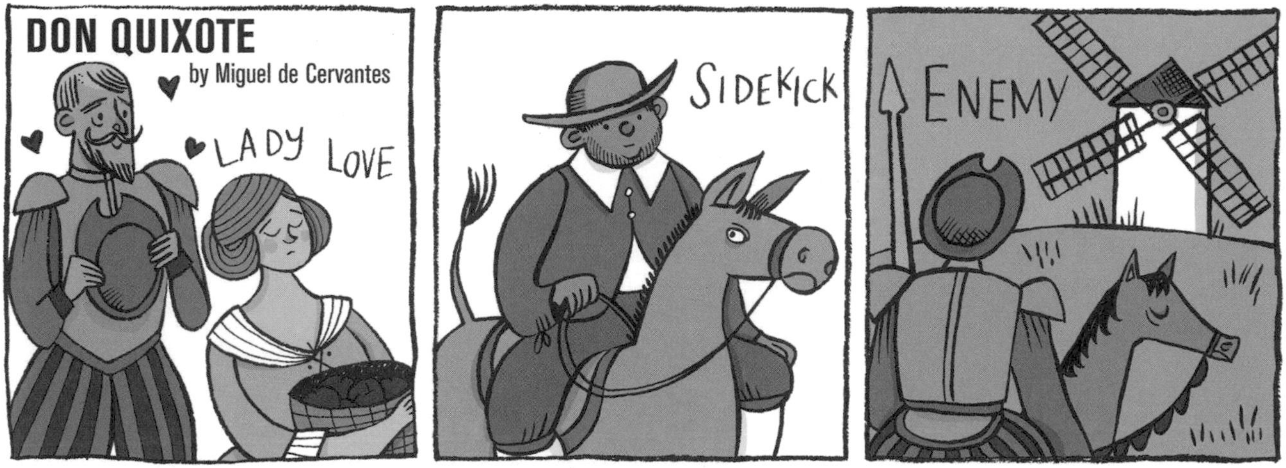
DON QUIXOTE
by Miguel de Cervantes
LADY LOVE
SIDEKICK
ENEMY

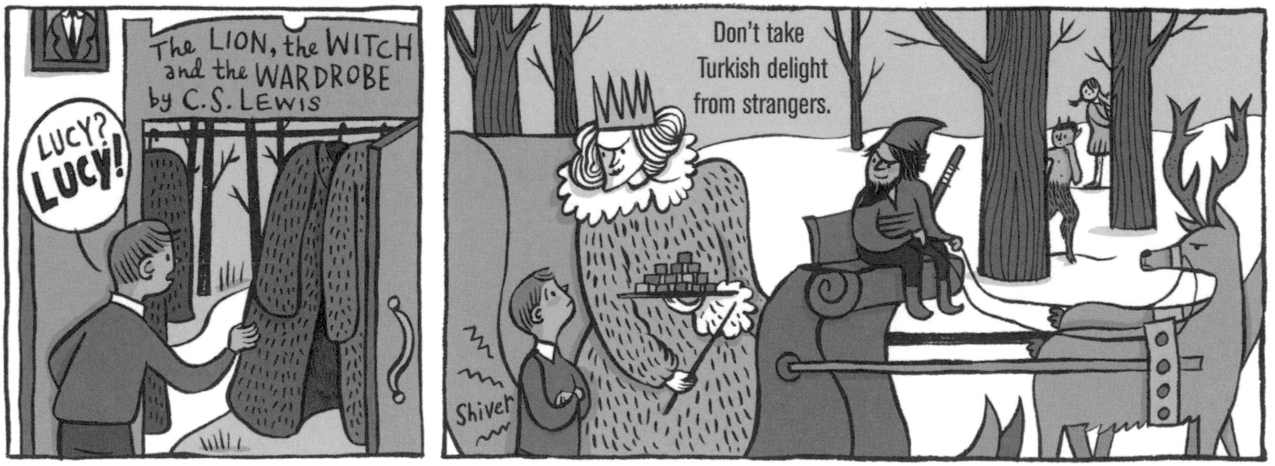
The LION, the WITCH and the WARDROBE
by C.S. LEWIS
LUCY? LUCY!
Don't take Turkish delight from strangers.
Shiver

SEE "FAMILIES"

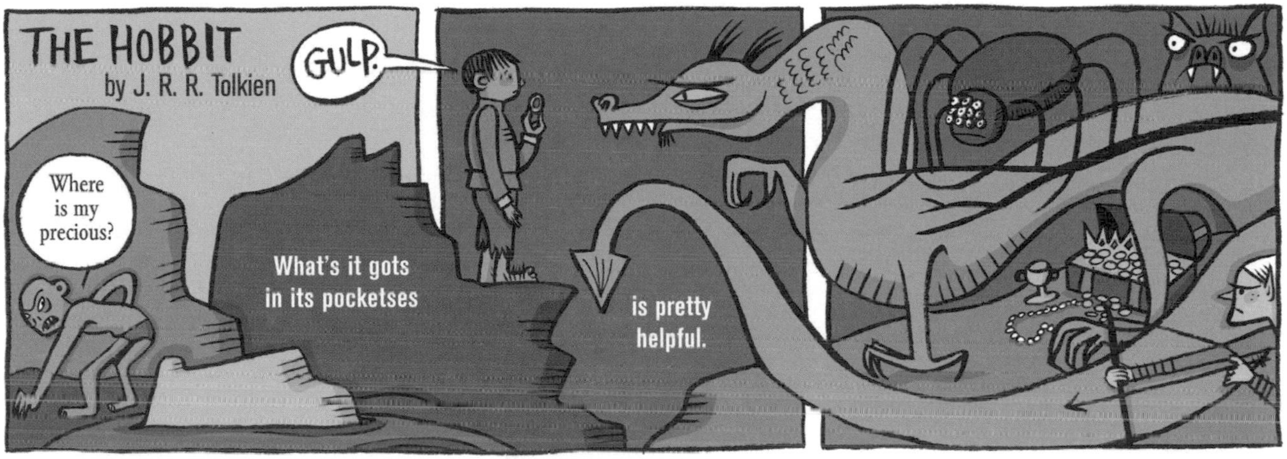
THE HOBBIT
by J. R. R. Tolkien
GULP.
Where is my precious?
What's it gots in its pocketses
is pretty helpful.

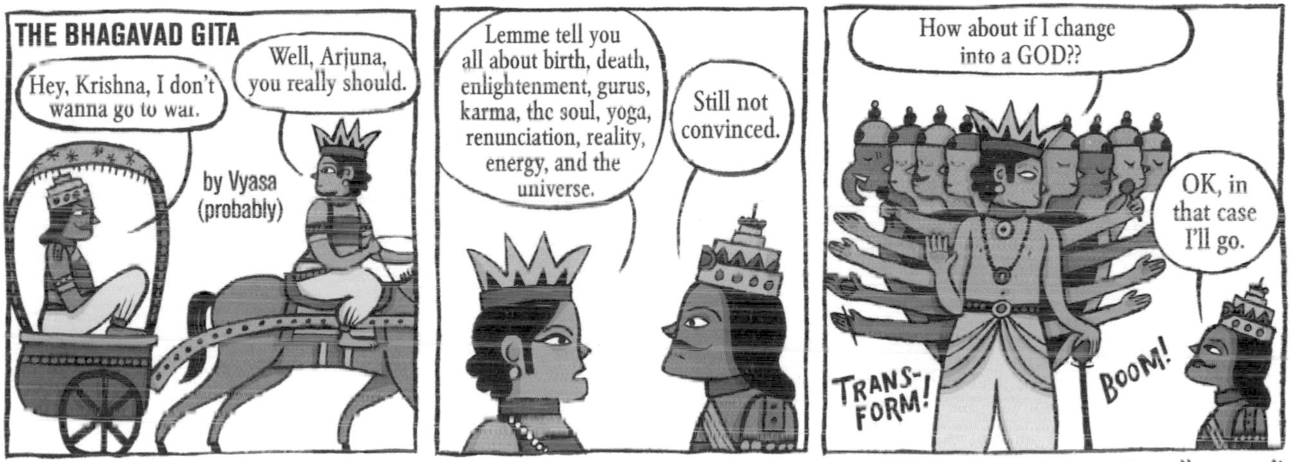
THE BHAGAVAD GITA
Hey, Krishna, I don't wanna go to war.
Well, Arjuna, you really should.
by Vyasa (probably)
Lemme tell you all about birth, death, enlightenment, gurus, karma, the soul, yoga, renunciation, reality, energy, and the universe.
Still not convinced.
How about if I change into a GOD??
OK, in that case I'll go.
TRANS-FORM!
BOOM!

SEE "WAR"

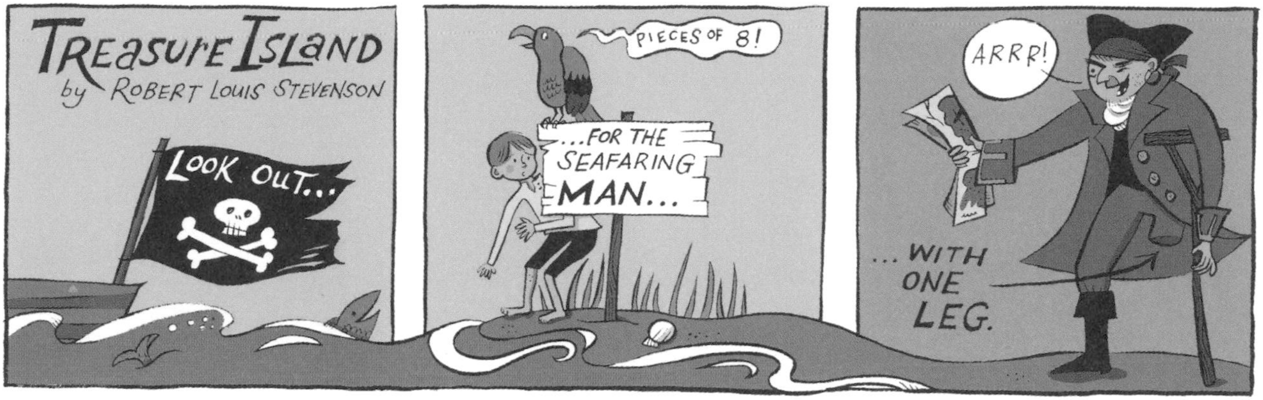
TREASURE ISLAND
by ROBERT LOUIS STEVENSON
LOOK OUT...
PIECES OF 8!
...FOR THE SEAFARING MAN...
ARRR!
...WITH ONE LEG.

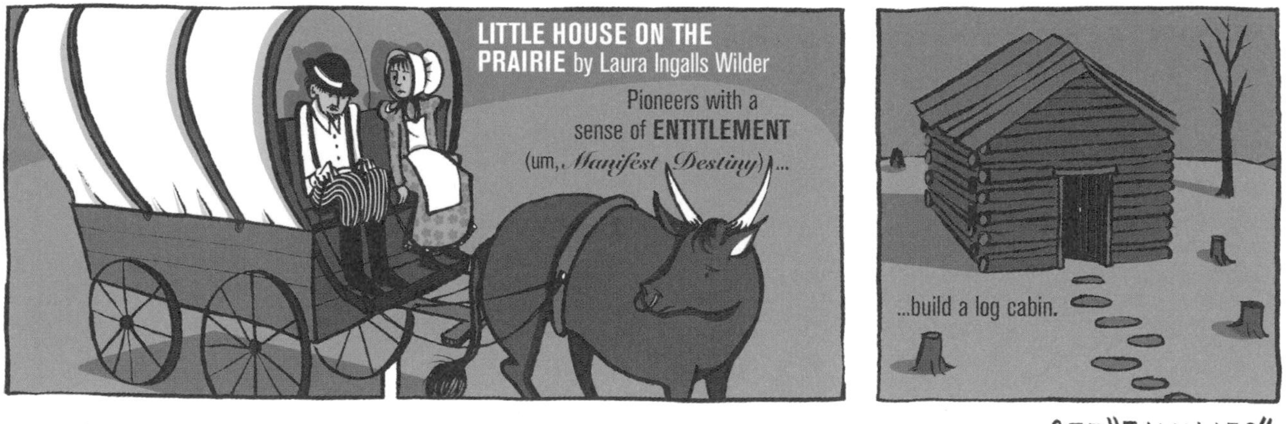
LITTLE HOUSE ON THE PRAIRIE by Laura Ingalls Wilder
Pioneers with a sense of ENTITLEMENT
(um, Manifest Destiny)...
...build a log cabin.

SEE "FAMILIES"

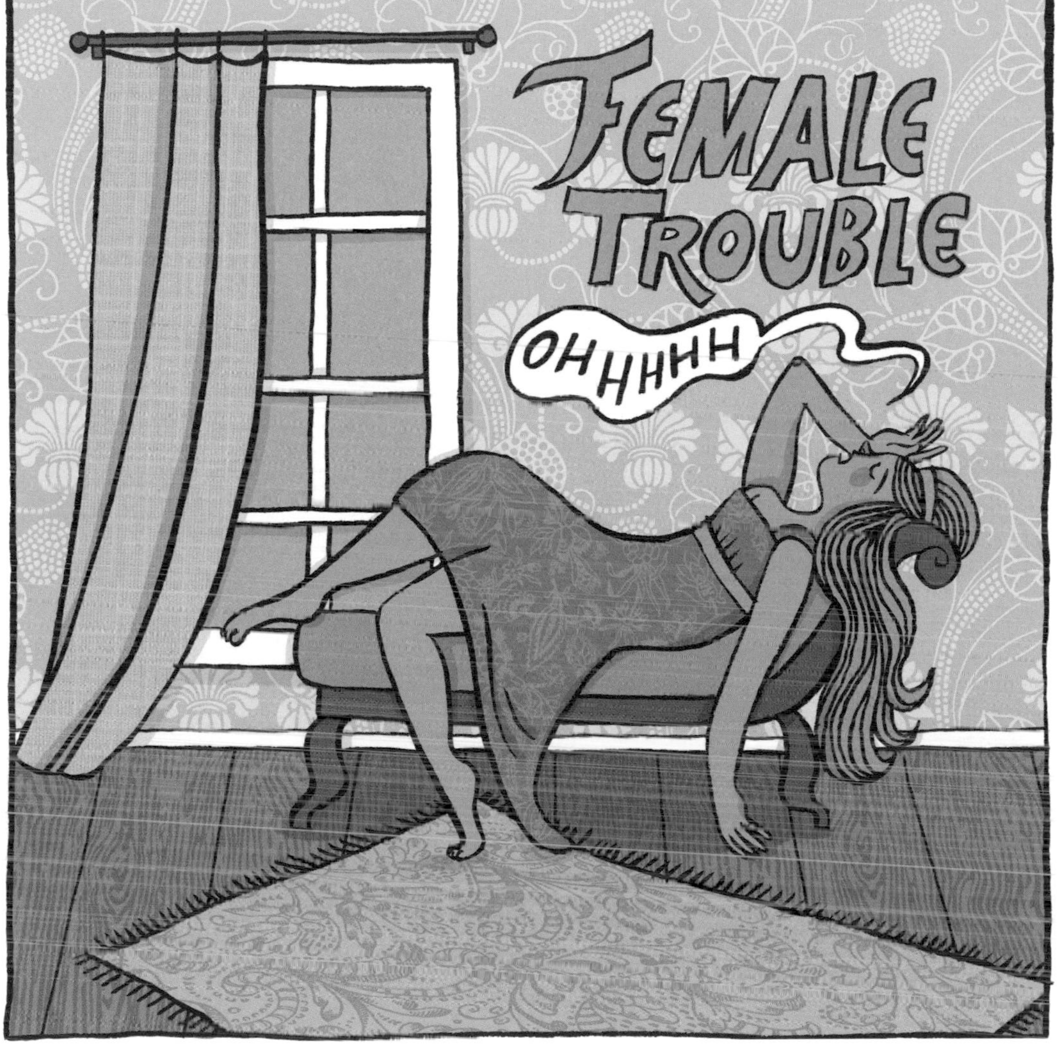
FEMALE TROUBLE
OHHHHH

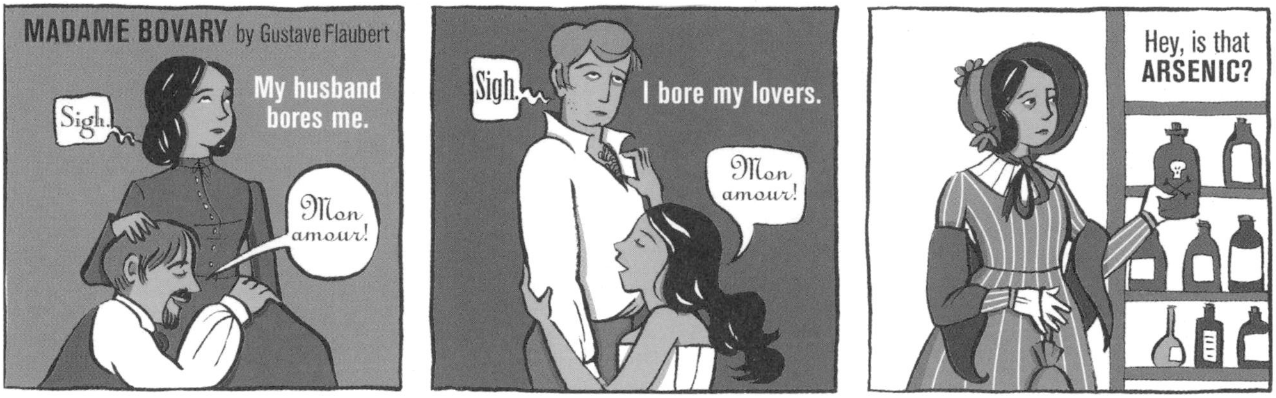
MADAME BOVARY by Gustave Flaubert
Sigh.
My husband bores me.
Mon amour!
Sigh.
I bore my lovers.
Mon amour!
Hey, is that ARSENIC?

SEE "SEX"

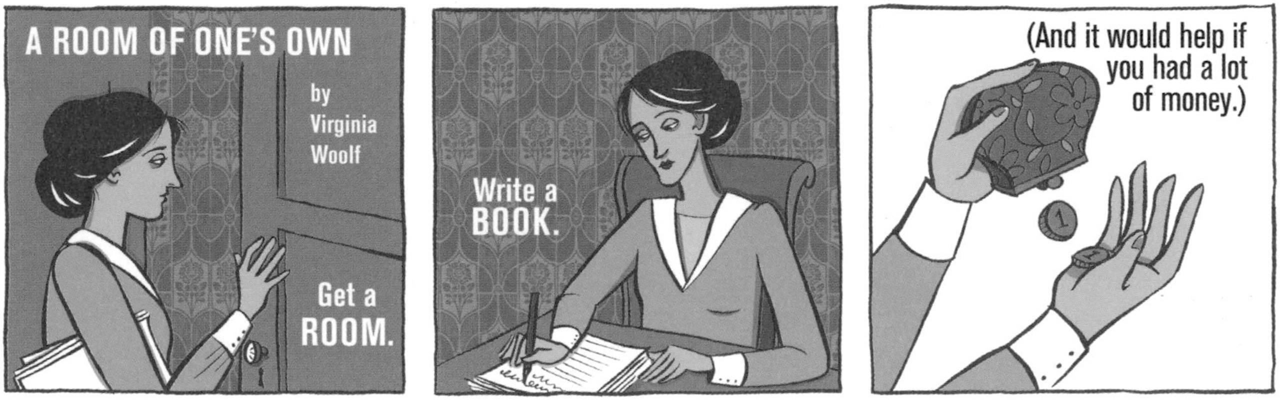
A ROOM OF ONE'S OWN
by Virginia Woolf
Get a ROOM.
Write a BOOK.
(And it would help if you had a lot of money.)

SEE "THOUGHTS"

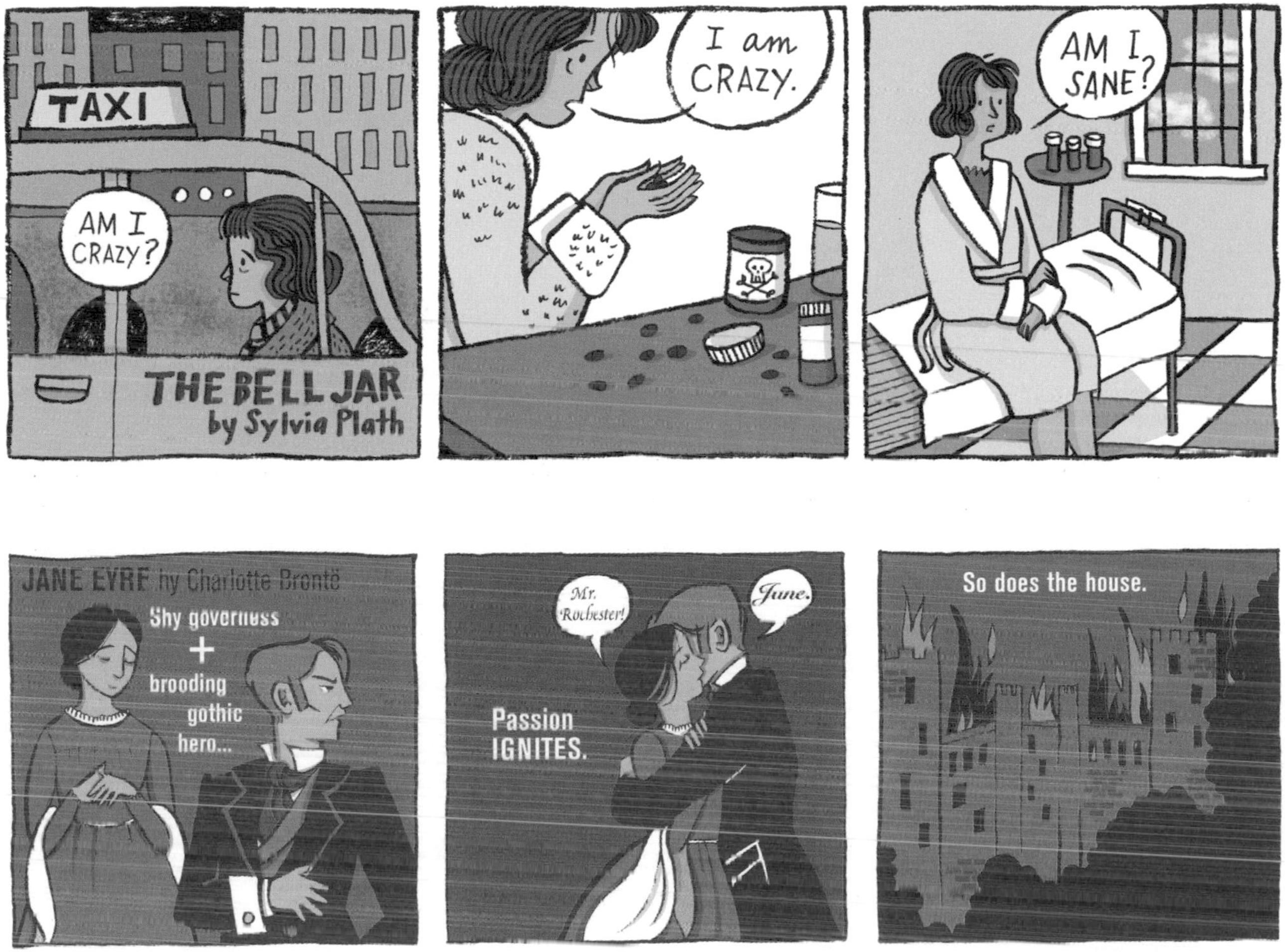
TAXI
AM I CRAZY?
THE BELL JAR
by Sylvia Plath
I am CRAZY.
AM I SANE?
JANE EYRE by Charlotte Brontë
Shy governess
+
brooding gothic hero...
Mr. Rochester!
Jane.
Passion IGNITES.
So does the house.

SEE "HORROR"

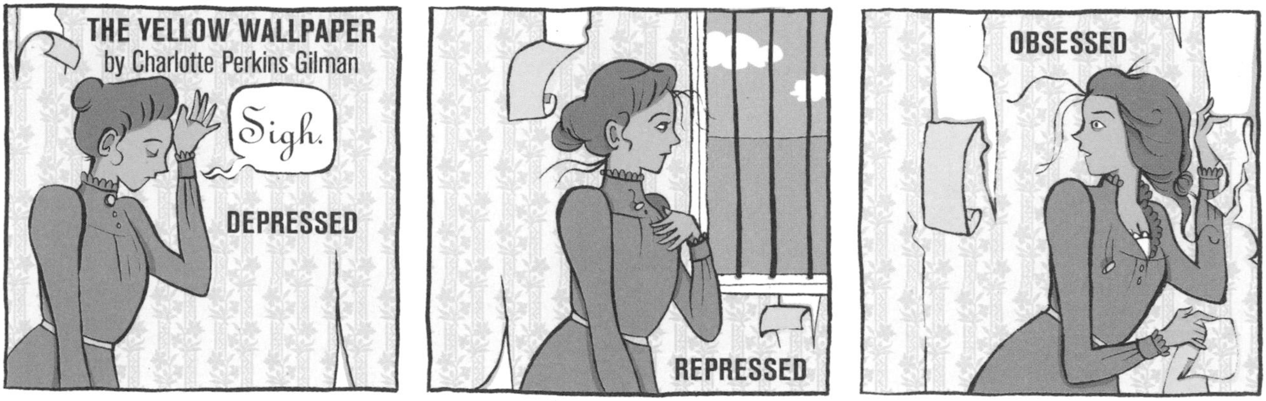
THE YELLOW WALLPAPER
by Charlotte Perkins Gilman
Sigh.
DEPRESSED
REPRESSED
OBSESSED

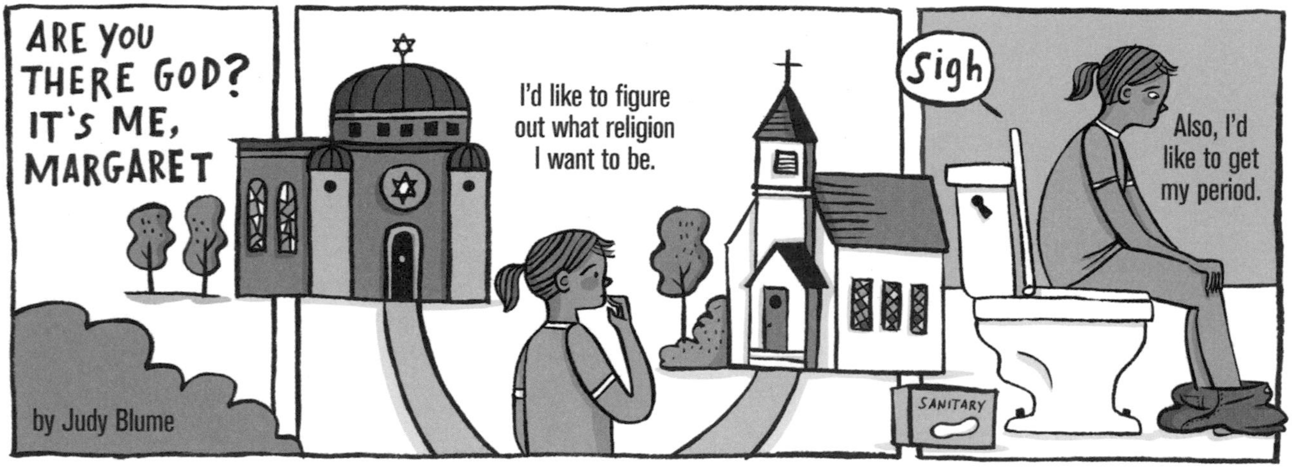
ARE YOU THERE GOD? IT'S ME, MARGARET
by Judy Blume
I'd like to figure out what religion I want to be.
Sigh
Also, I'd like to get my period.
SANITARY

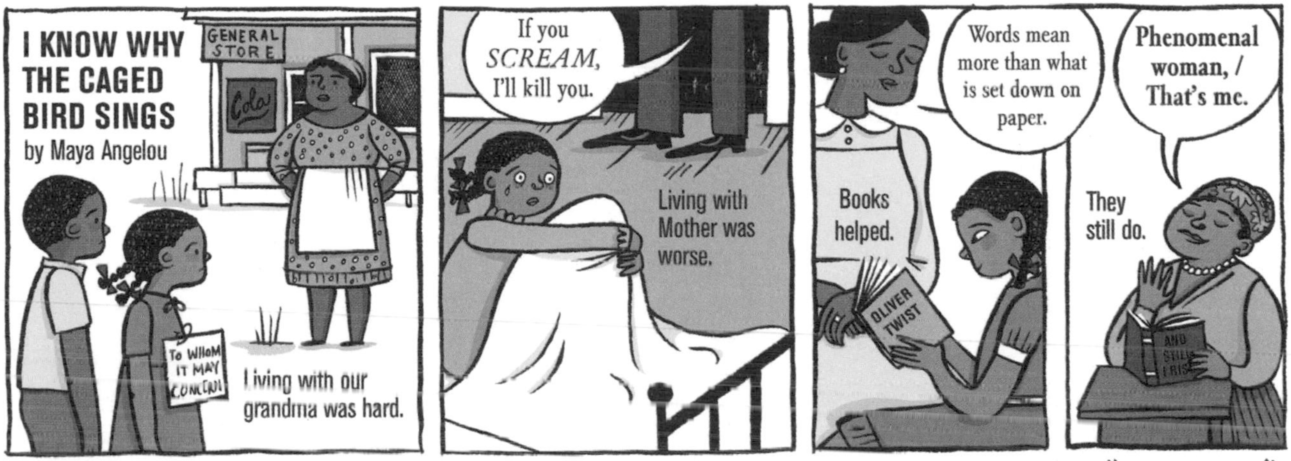
I KNOW WHY THE CAGED BIRD SINGS
by Maya Angelou
GENERAL STORE
Cola
To WHOM IT MAY
Living with our grandma was hard.
If you *SCREAM*, I'll kill you.
Living with Mother was worse.
Books helped.
Words mean more than what is set down on paper.
OLIVER TWIST
They still do.
Phenomenal woman, / That's me.

SEE "FAMILIES"

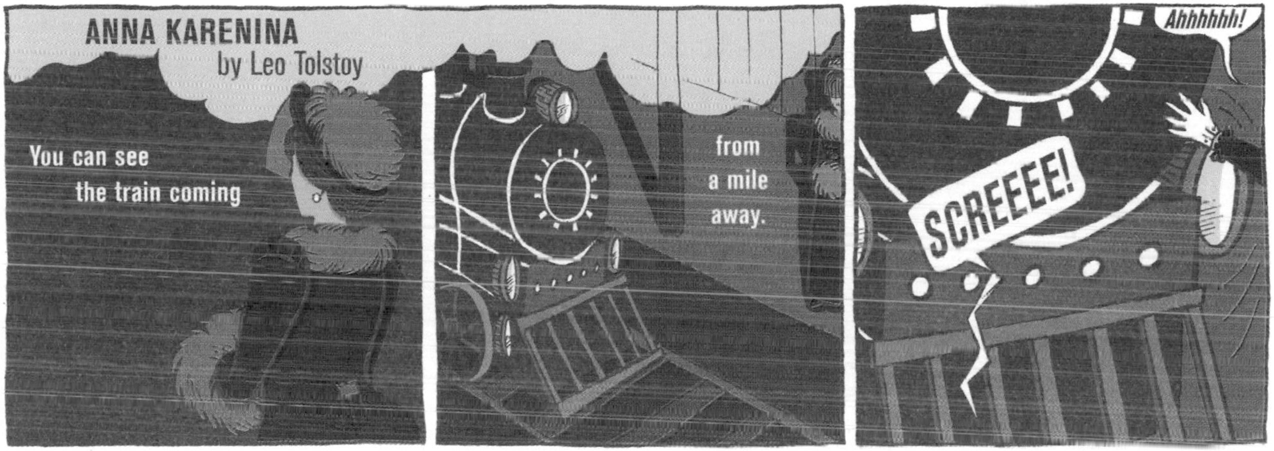
ANNA KARENINA
by Leo Tolstoy
You can see the train coming
from a mile away.
Ahhhhhh!
SCREEEE!

SEE "LOVE," "SEX," "DEATH"

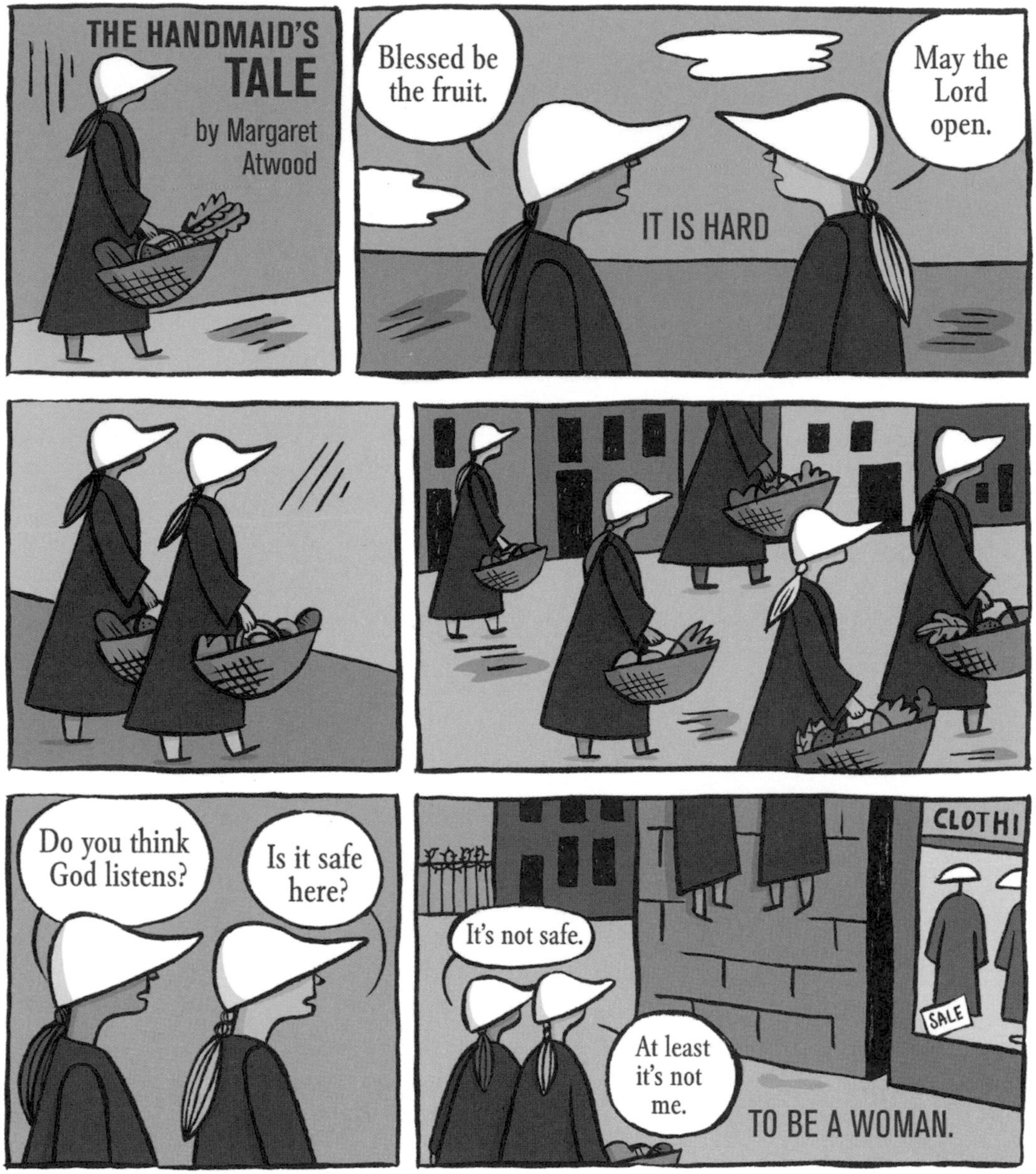
THE HANDMAID'S
TALE
by Margaret
Atwood
Blessed be the fruit.
May the Lord open.
IT IS HARD
Do you think God listens?
Is it safe here?
CLOTHI
SALE
It's not safe.
At least it's not me.
TO BE A WOMAN.

SEE "HORROR"

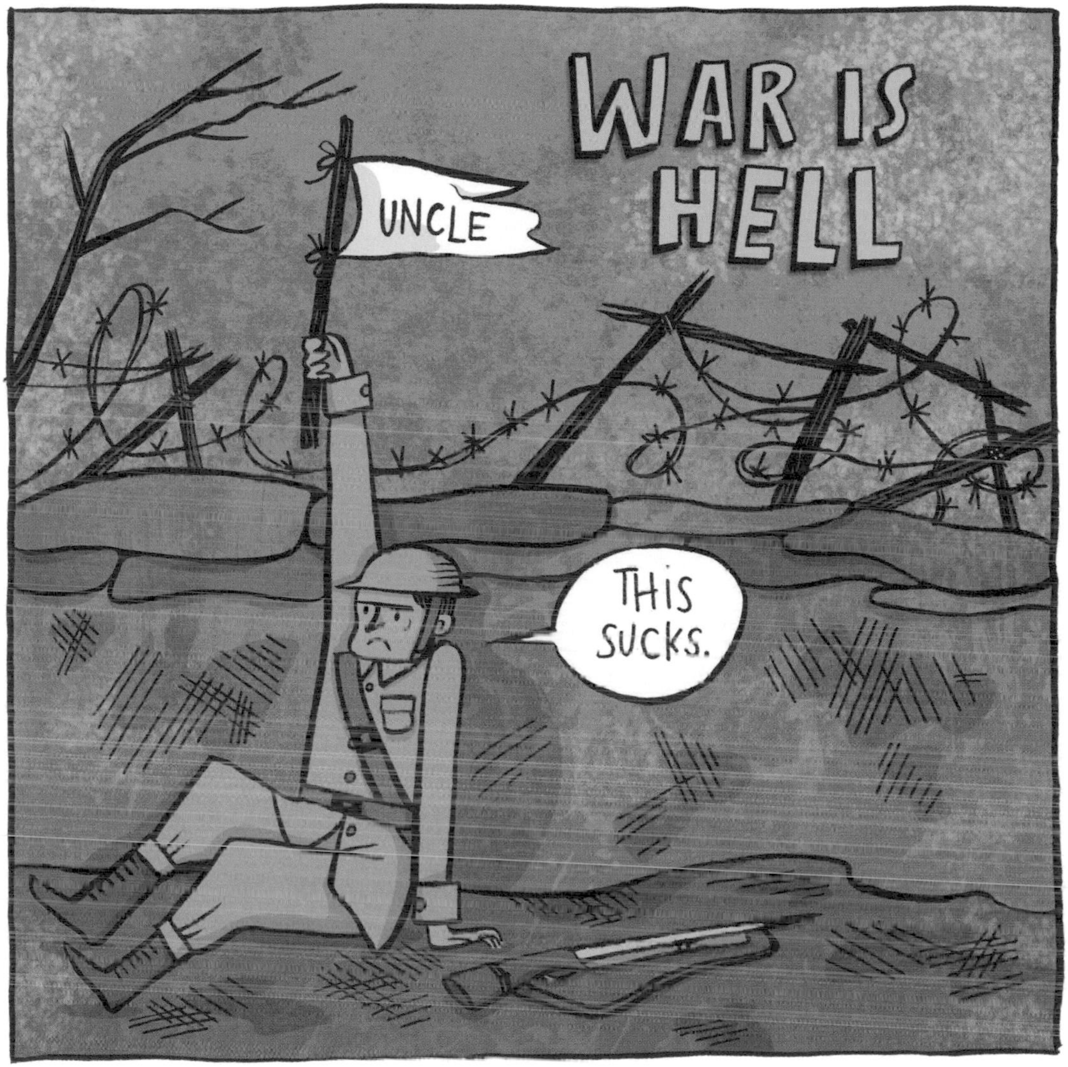
WAR IS HELL
UNCLE
THIS SUCKS.

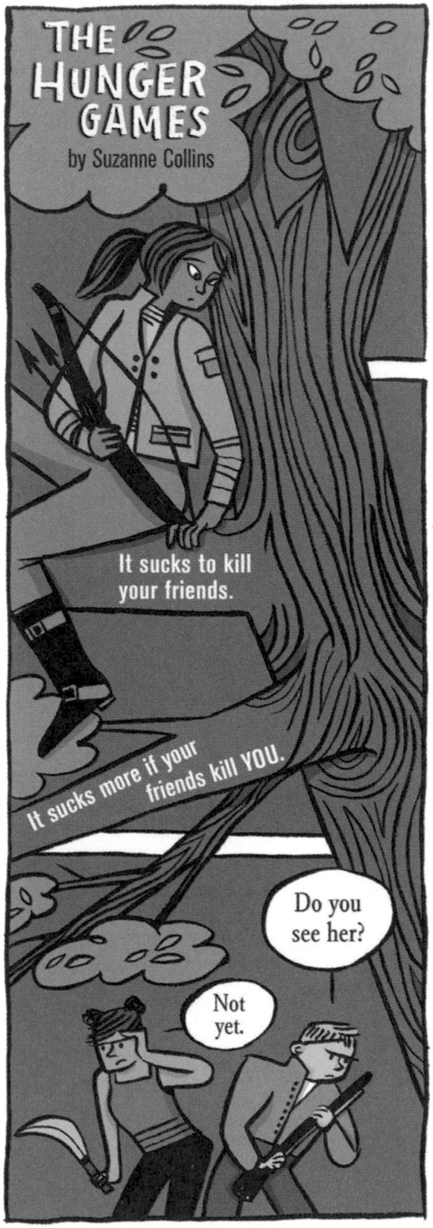
THE HUNGER GAMES
by Suzanne Collins
It sucks to kill your friends.
It sucks more if your friends kill YOU.
Do you see her?
Not yet.

SEE "DEATH"

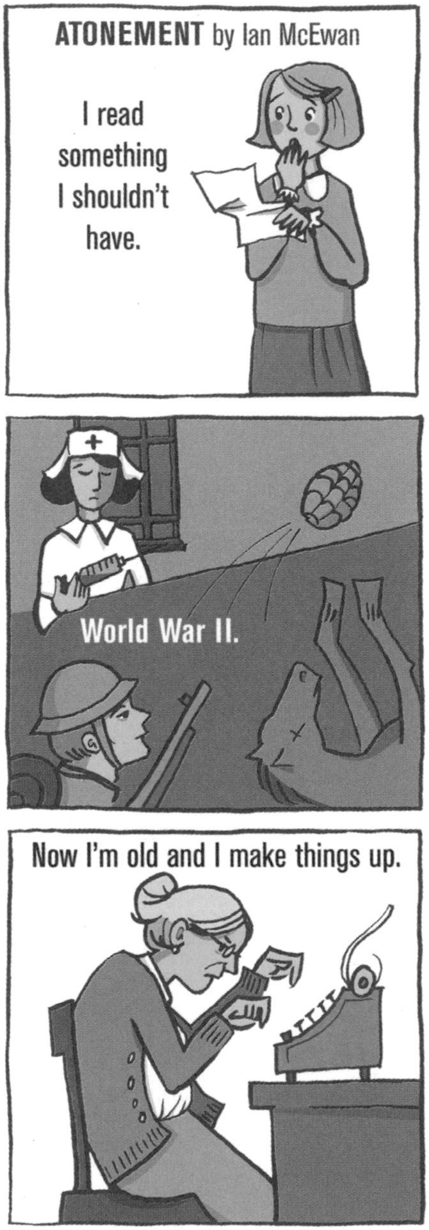
ATONEMENT by Ian McEwan
I read something I shouldn't have.
World War II.
Now I'm old and I make things up.

SEE "DEATH"

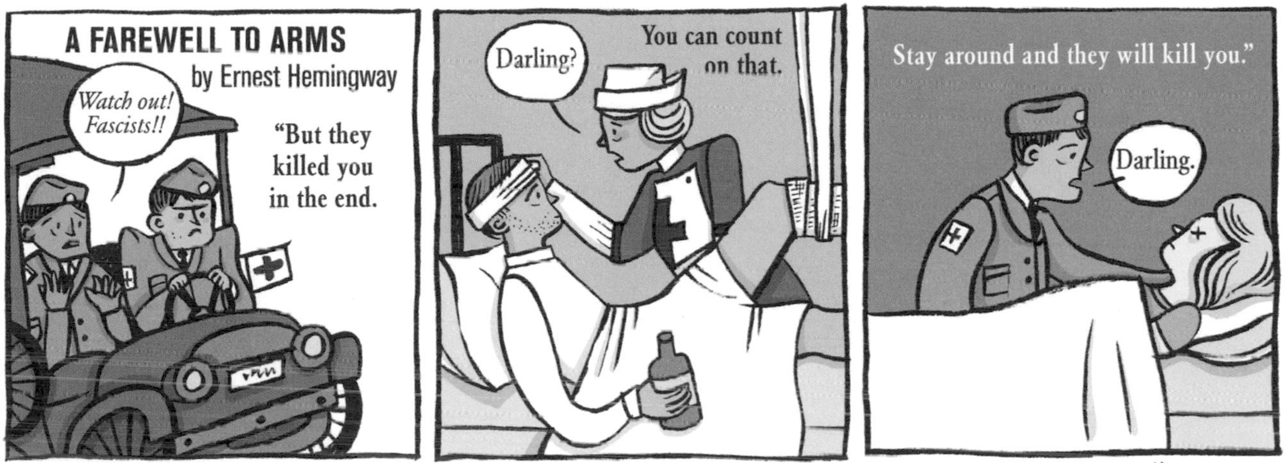
A FAREWELL TO ARMS
by Ernest Hemingway
Watch out! Fascists!!
"But they killed you in the end.
Darling?
You can count on that.
Stay around and they will kill you."
Darling.

SEE "DEATH"

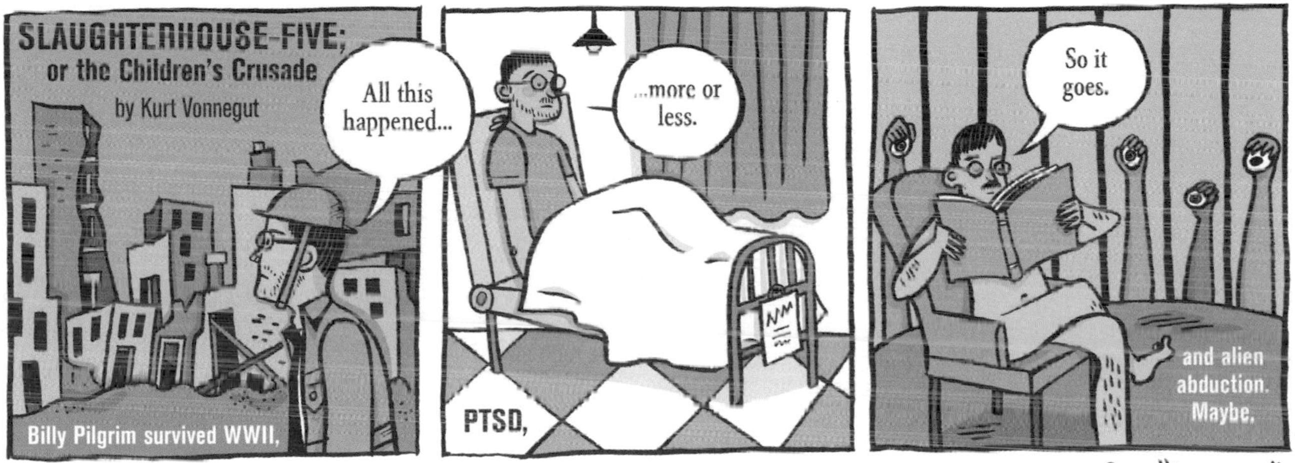
SLAUGHTERHOUSE-FIVE; or the Children's Crusade
by Kurt Vonnegut
All this happened...
Billy Pilgrim survived WWII,
...more or less.
PTSD,
So it goes.
and alien abduction. Maybe.

SEE "DEATH"

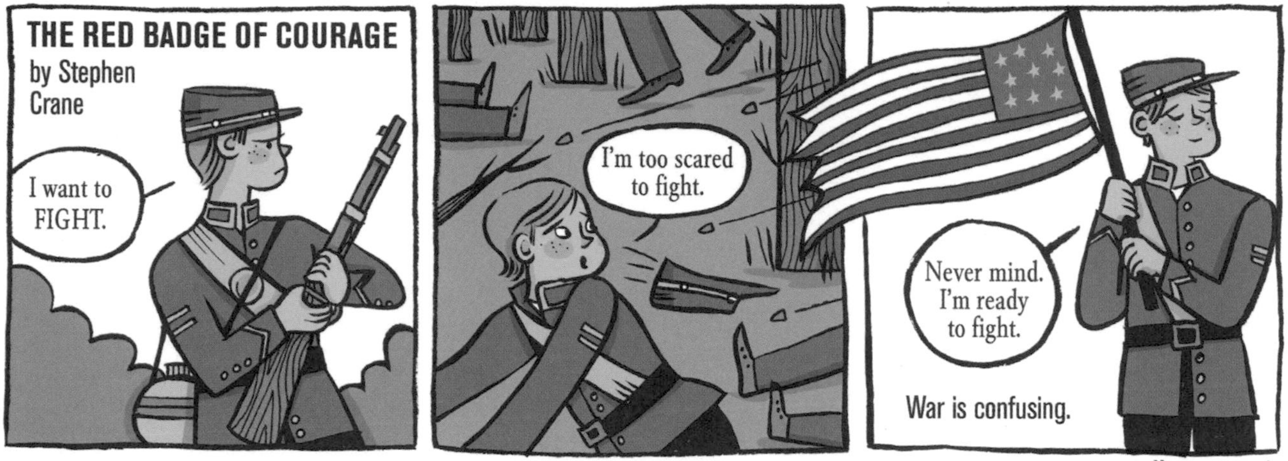
THE RED BADGE OF COURAGE
by Stephen Crane
I want to FIGHT.
I'm too scared to fight.
Never mind. I'm ready to fight.
War is confusing.

SEE "DEATH"

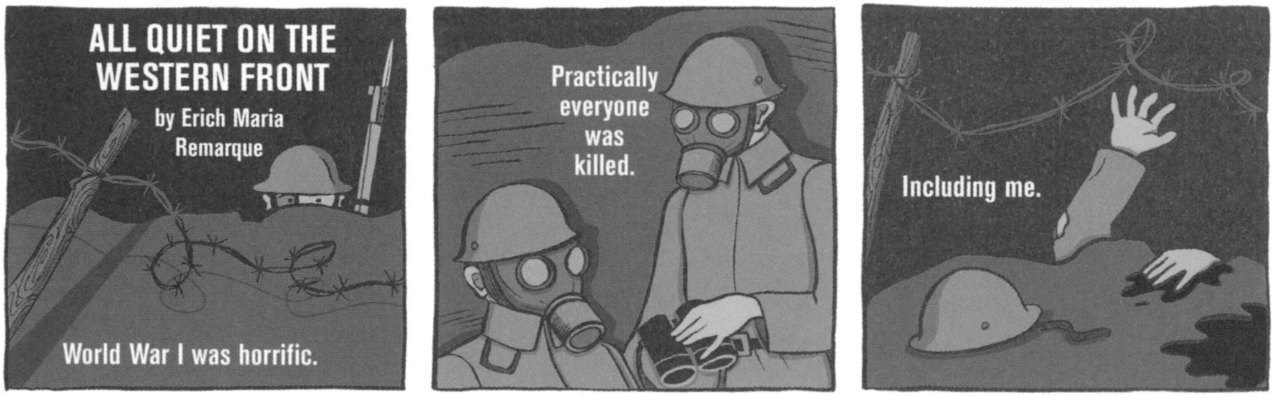
ALL QUIET ON THE WESTERN FRONT
by Erich Maria Remarque
World War I was horrific.
Practically everyone was killed.
Including me.

SEE "DEATH"

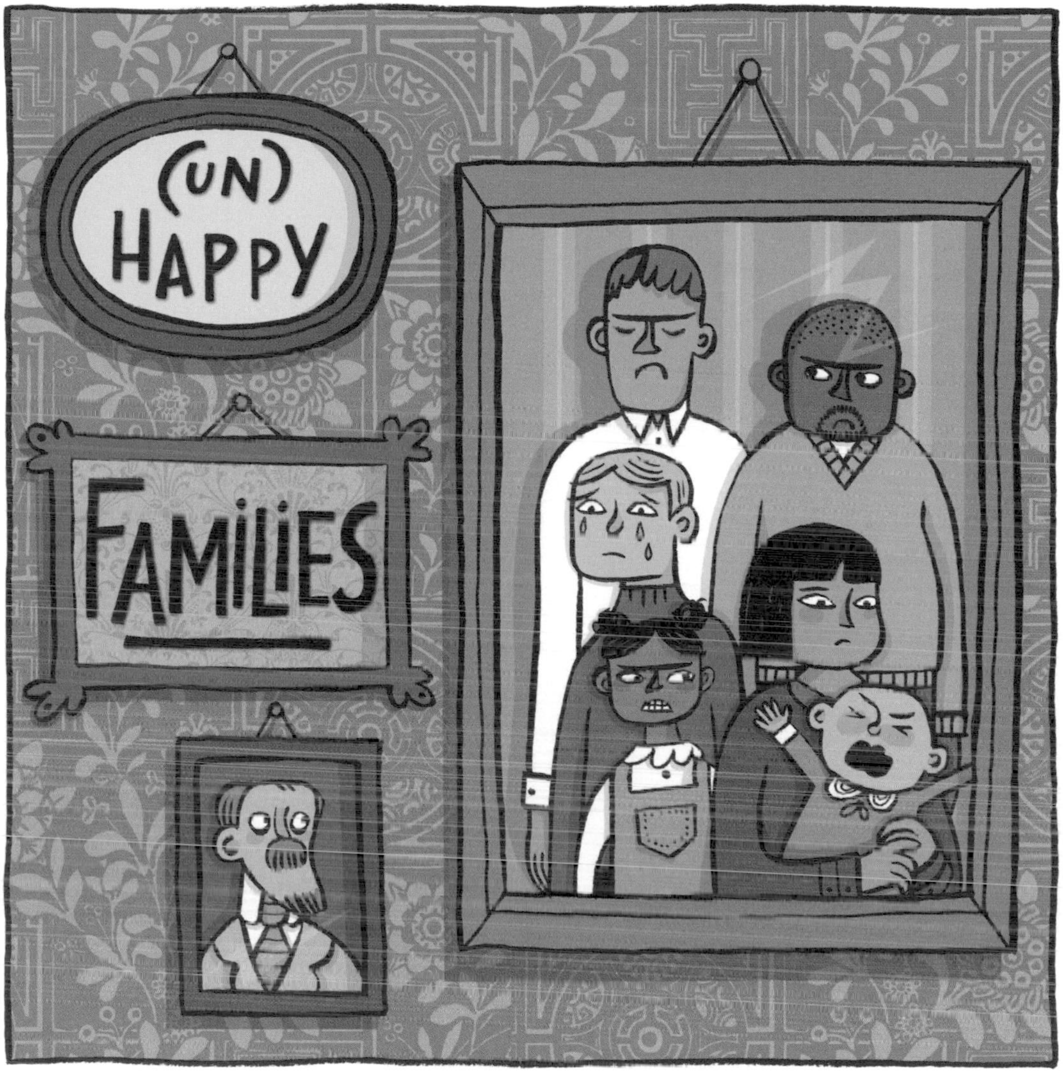
(UN) HAPPY
FAMILIES

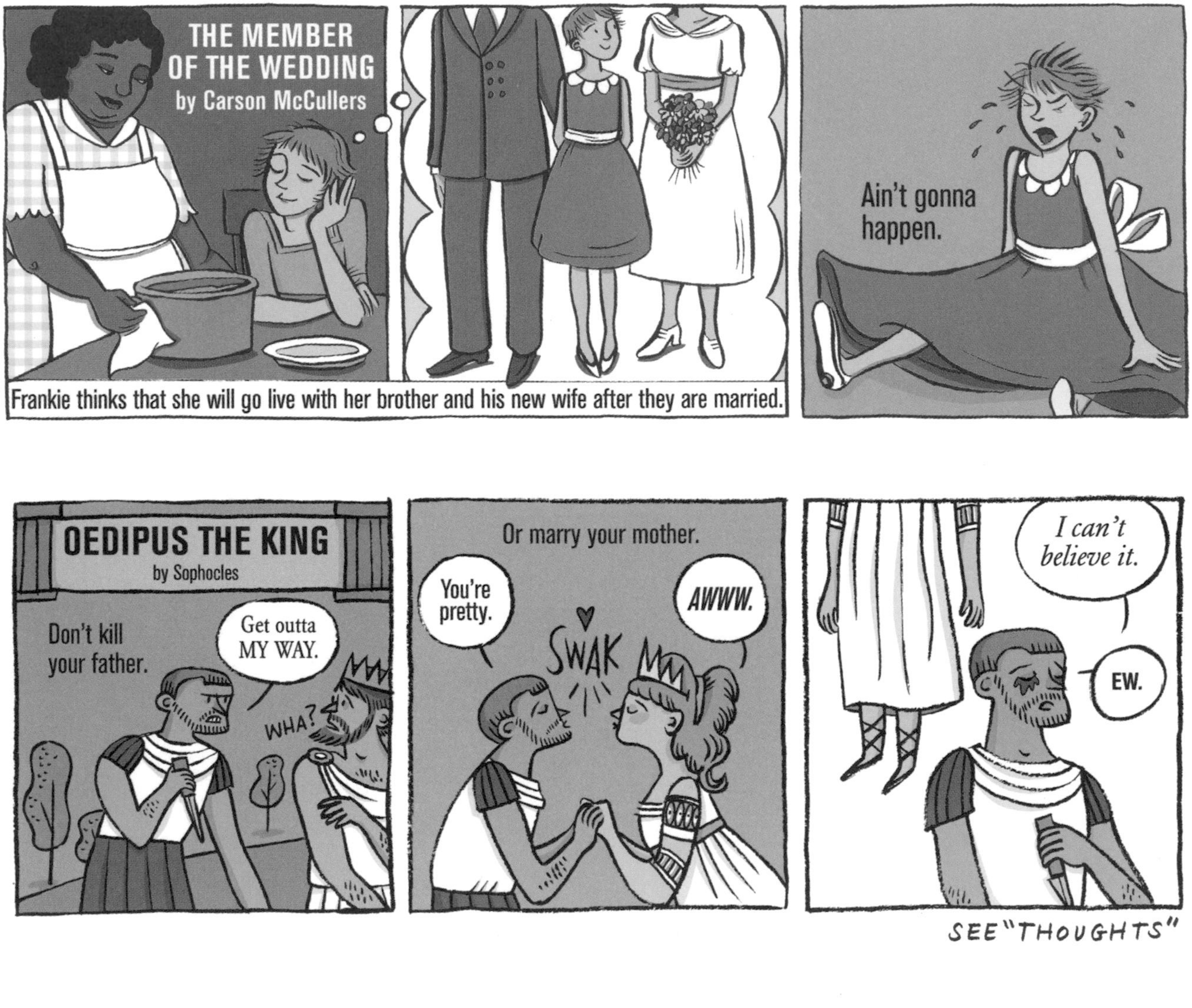
THE MEMBER OF THE WEDDING
by Carson McCullers
Frankie thinks that she will go live with her brother and his new wife after they are married.
Ain't gonna happen.
OEDIPUS THE KING
by Sophocles
Don't kill your father.
Get outta MY WAY.
WHA?
Or marry your mother.
You're pretty.
SWAK
AWWW.
I can't believe it.
EW.
SEE "THOUGHTS"

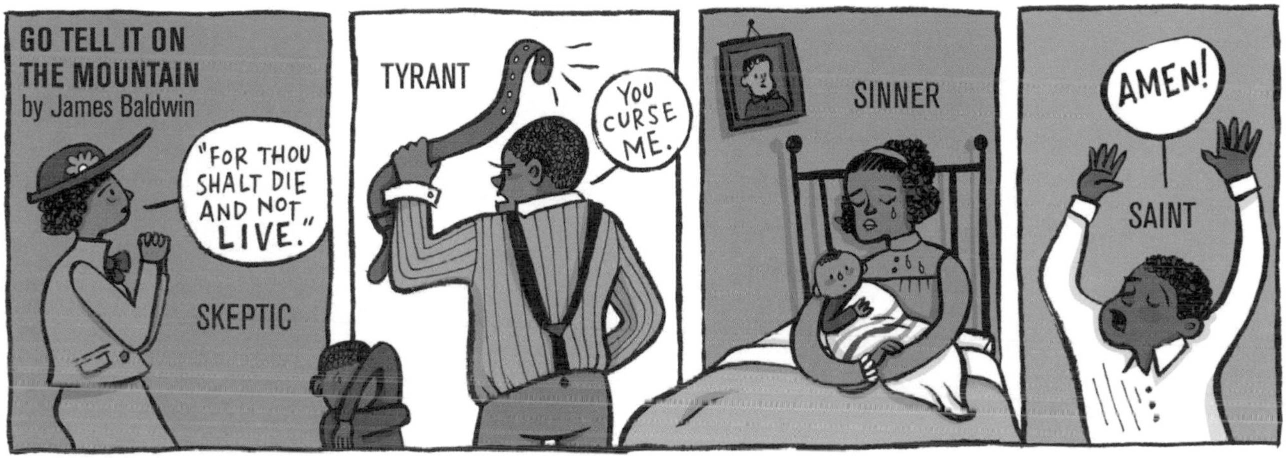
GO TELL IT ON THE MOUNTAIN
by James Baldwin
"FOR THOU SHALT DIE AND NOT LIVE."
SKEPTIC
TYRANT
YOU CURSE ME.
SINNER
AMEN!
SAINT

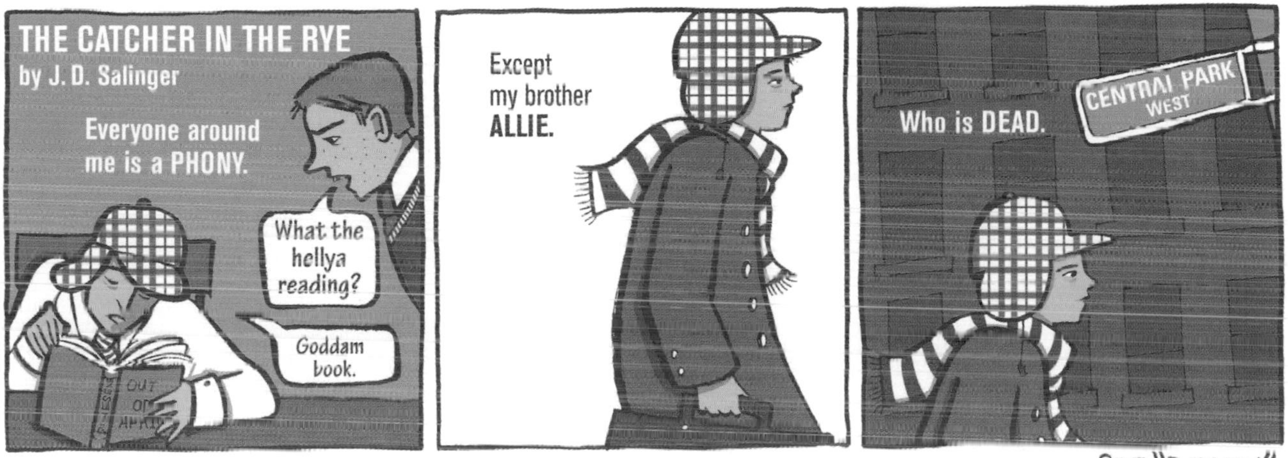
THE CATCHER IN THE RYE
by J. D. Salinger
Everyone around me is a PHONY.
What the hellya reading?
Goddam book.
Except my brother ALLIE.
Who is DEAD.
CENTRAL PARK
WEST

SEE "DEATH"

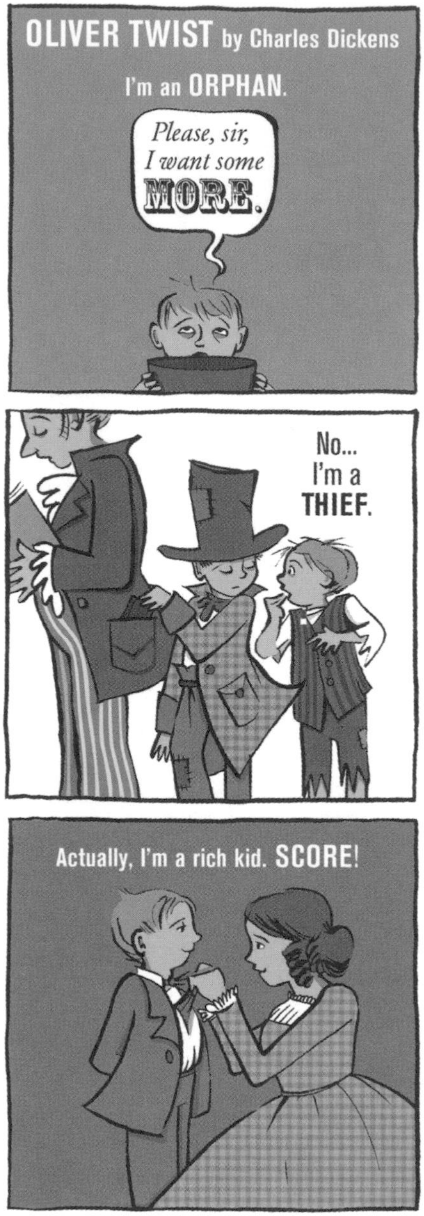
OLIVER TWIST by Charles Dickens
I'm an ORPHAN.
Please, sir, I want some MORE.
No... I'm a THIEF.
Actually, I'm a rich kid. SCORE!

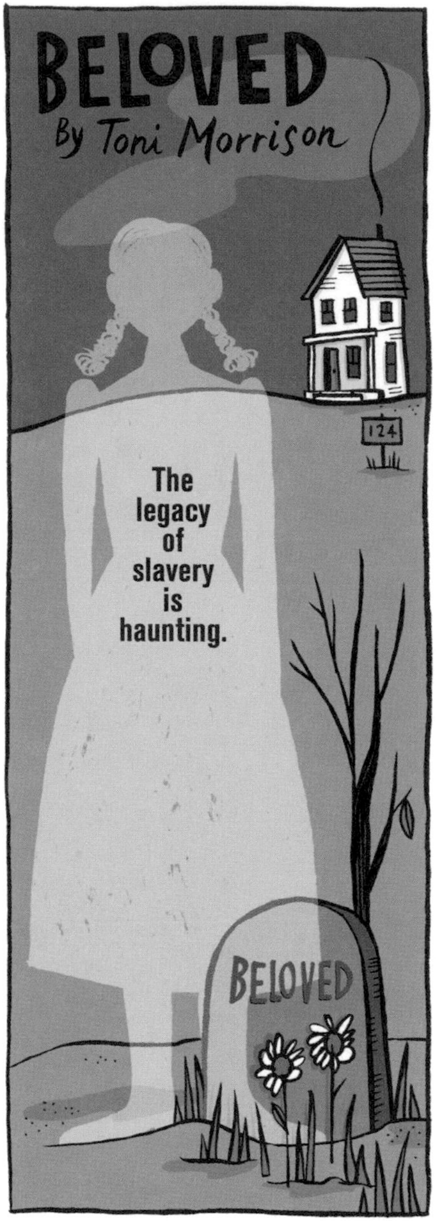
BELOVED
By Toni Morrison
124
The legacy of slavery is haunting.
BELOVED

SEE "DEATH"

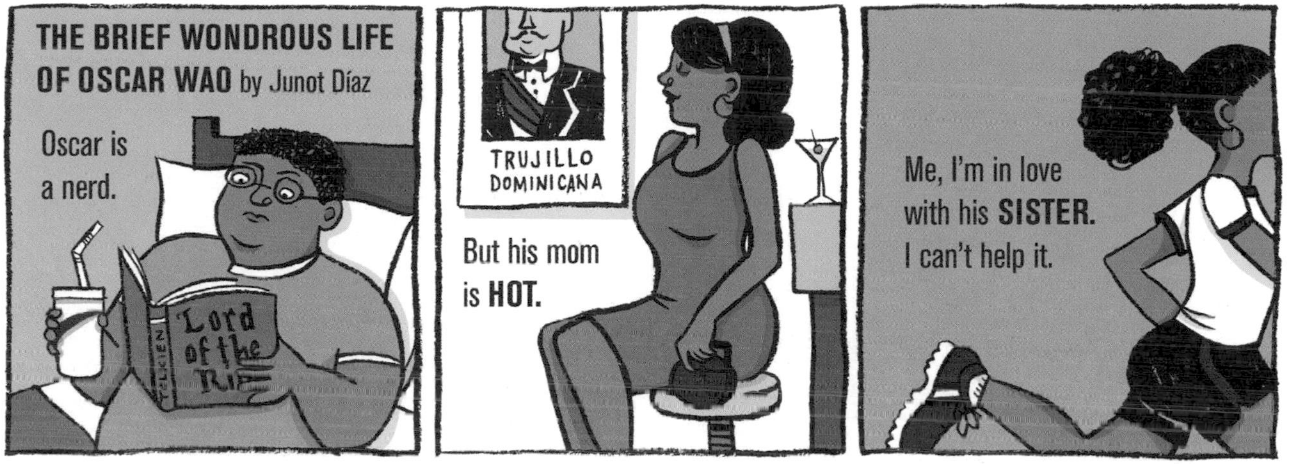
THE BRIEF WONDROUS LIFE OF OSCAR WAO by Junot Díaz
Oscar is a nerd.
Lord of the Ri
TOLKIEN
TRUJILLO DOMINICANA
But his mom is HOT.
Me, I'm in love with his SISTER. I can't help it.

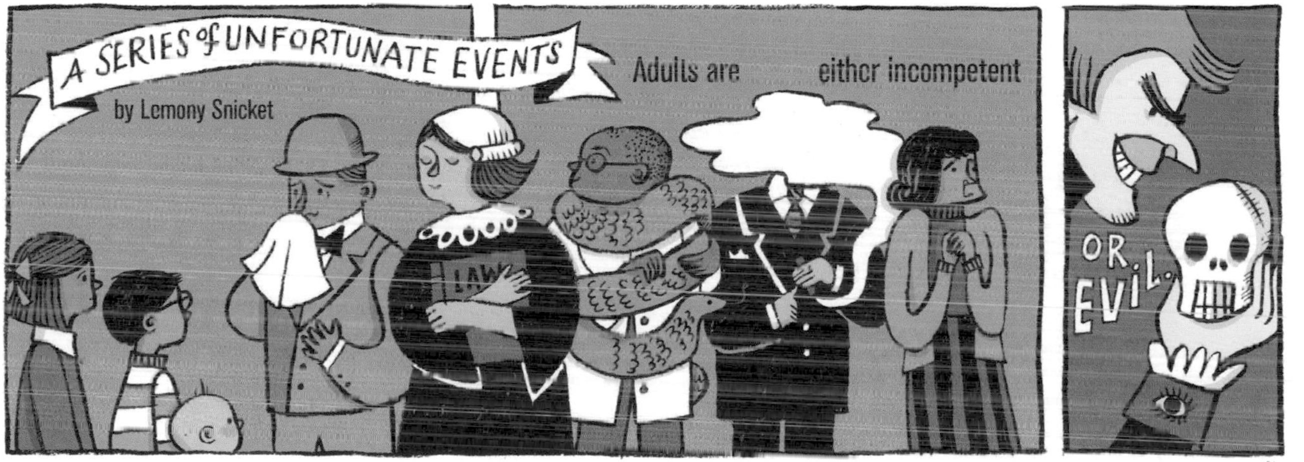
A SERIES of UNFORTUNATE EVENTS
by Lemony Snicket
Adults are
either incompetent
LAW
OR EVIL.

SEE "THOUGHTS"

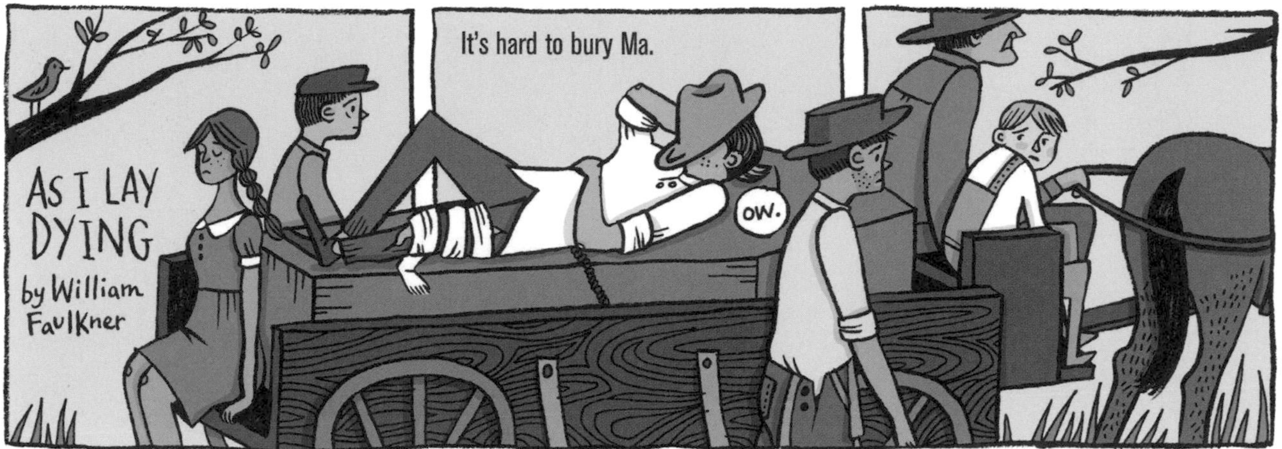
AS I LAY DYING
by William Faulkner
It's hard to bury Ma.
OW.

SEE "DEATH"

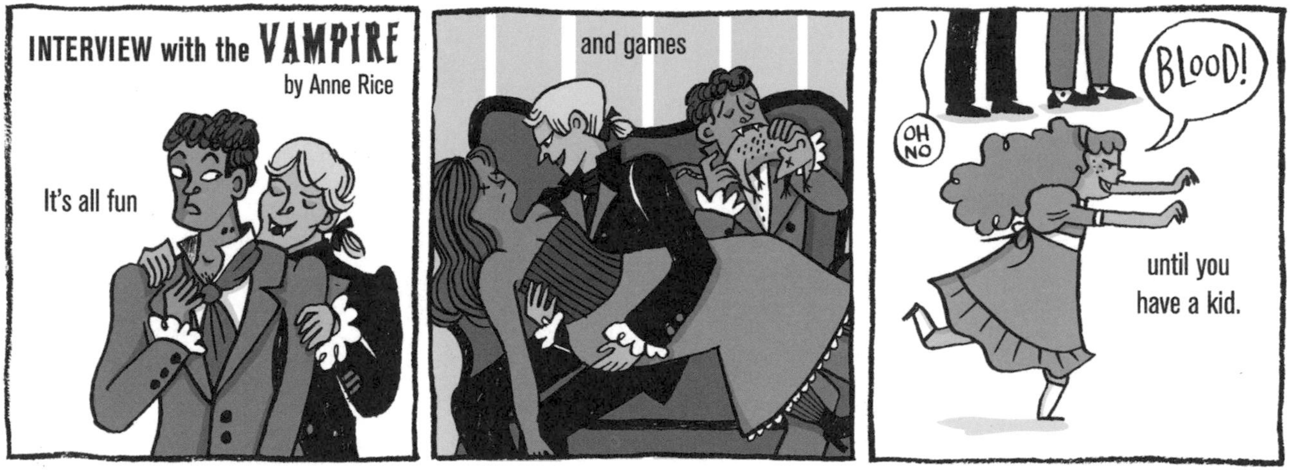
INTERVIEW with the VAMPIRE
by Anne Rice
It's all fun
and games
OH NO
BLOOD!
until you have a kid.

SEE "HORROR"

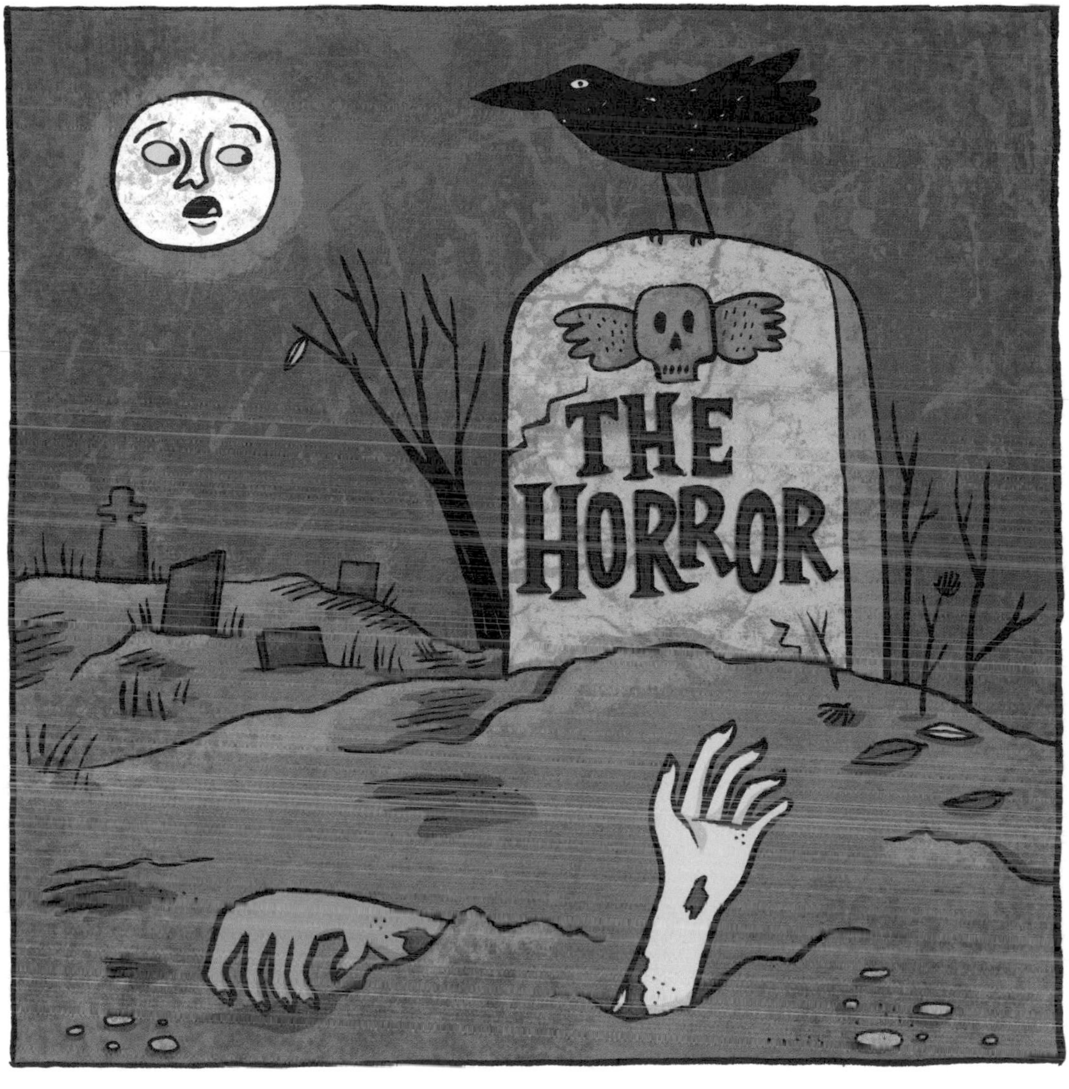
THE HORROR

HEART OF DARKNESS
by Joseph Conrad
AFRICA...
...drives white guys CRAZY.
The HORROR! The HORROR!

SEE "THOUGHTS"

WUTHERING HEIGHTS
by EMILY BRÖNTE
Huh?
LET ME IN!
CATHY IS A GHOST.
HEATHCLIFF IS A FIEND.
GRRRR I HAVE NO PITY.
Heathcliff!
CATHY! YOU'RE DRIVING ME CRAZY!
A MATCH MADE IN HELL.

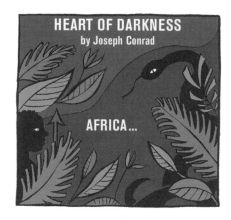

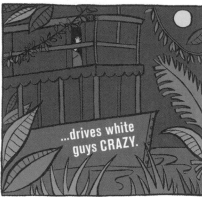

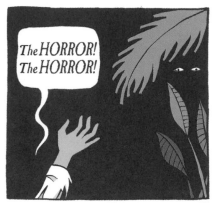

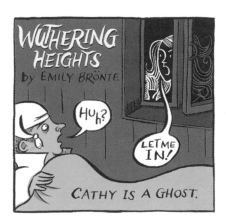

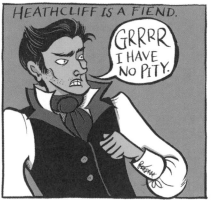

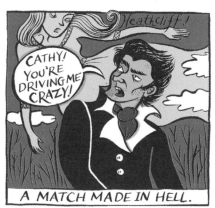

SEE "LOVE"

The
TURN
of the SCREW
BY HENRY JAMES,
A NOVEL
AS TOLD *in*
FEWER THAN
30 SECONDS

The GOVERNESS
SEES GHOSTS...

...OR
PERHAPS
SHE IS
Insane.

EITHER WAY,
IT'S QUITE SCARY.

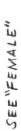

SEE "FEMALE"

31

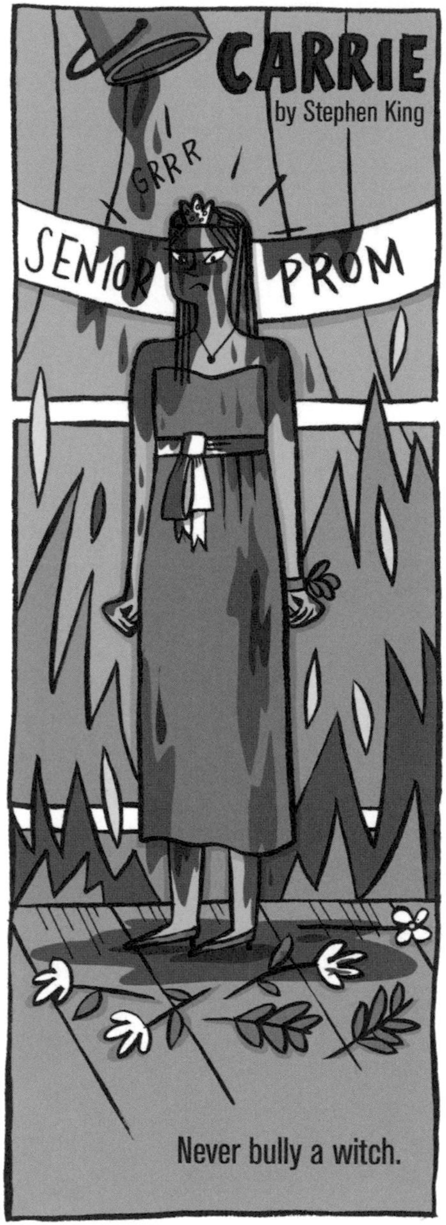
CARRIE
by Stephen King
GRRR
SENIOR PROM
Never bully a witch.

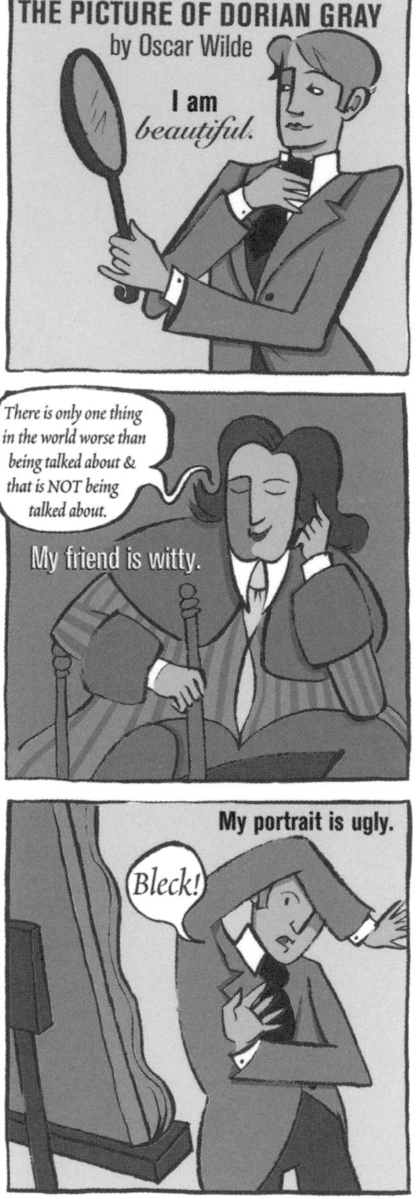
THE PICTURE OF DORIAN GRAY
by Oscar Wilde
I am
beautiful.
There is only one thing in the world worse than being talked about & that is NOT being talked about.
My friend is witty.
My portrait is ugly.
Bleck!

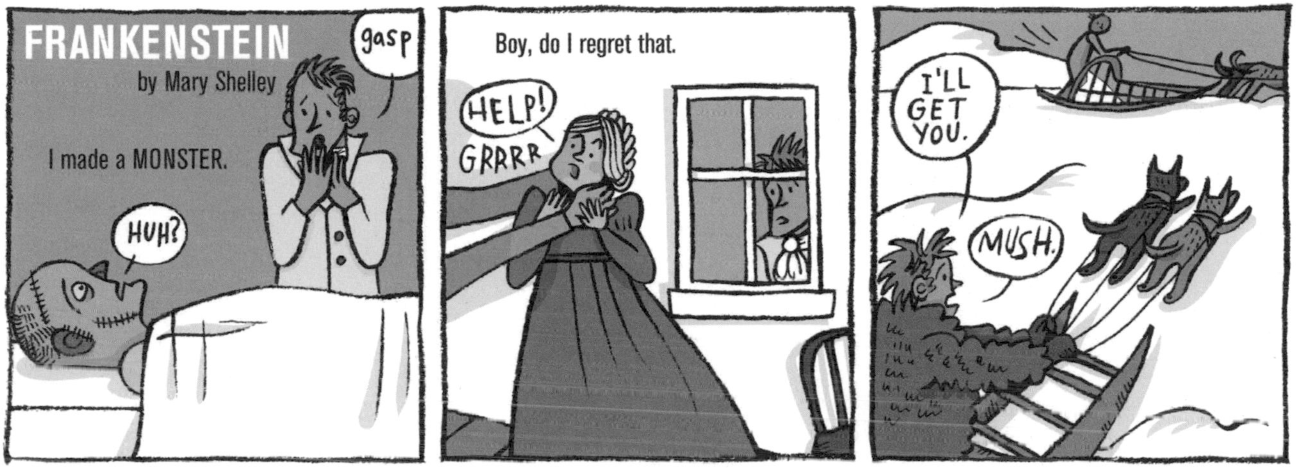
FRANKENSTEIN
by Mary Shelley
I made a MONSTER.
gasp
HUH?
Boy, do I regret that.
HELP!
GRRRR
I'LL GET YOU.
MUSH.

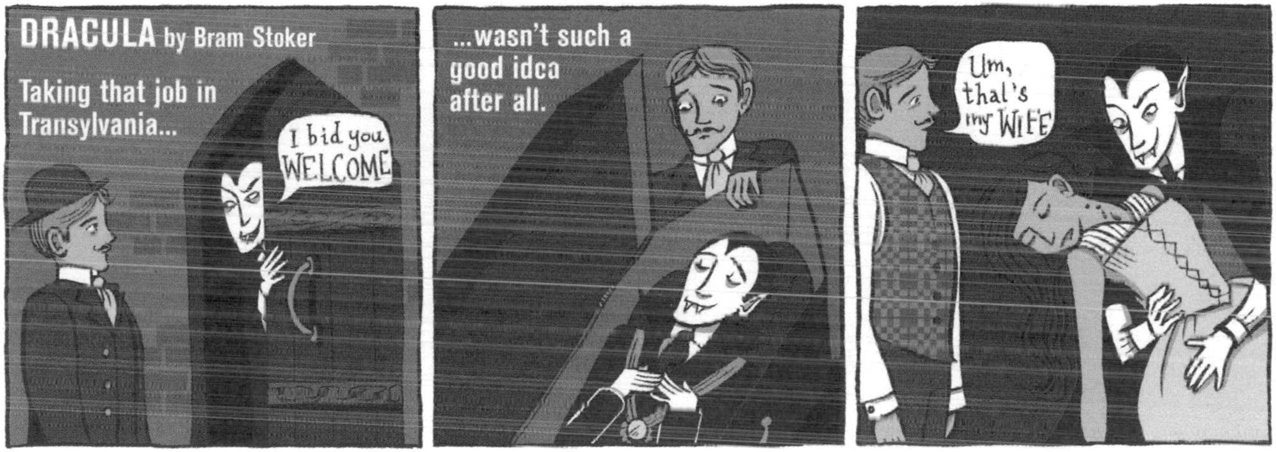
DRACULA by Bram Stoker
Taking that job in Transylvania...
I bid you WELCOME
...wasn't such a good idea after all.
Um, that's my WIFE

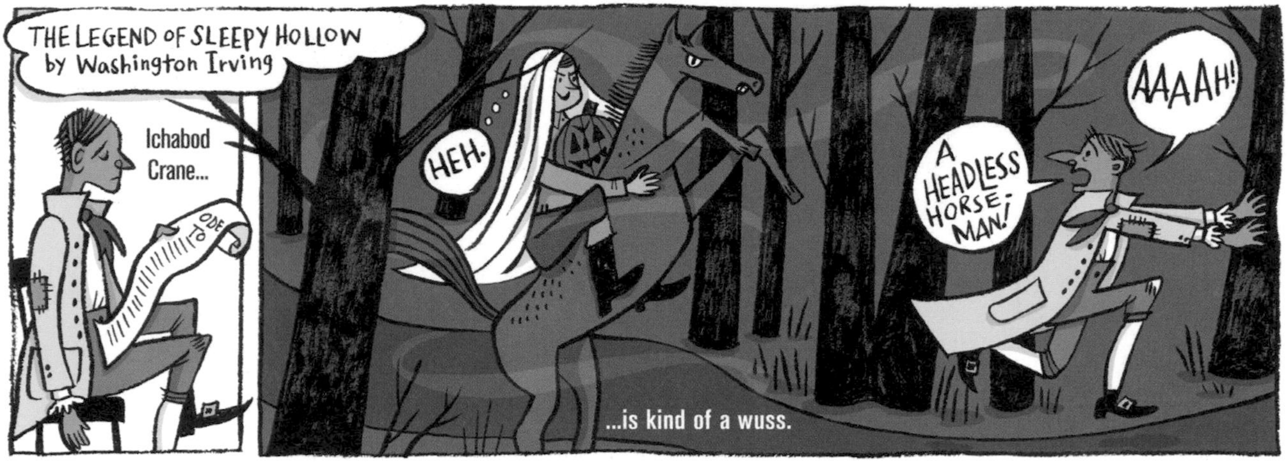
THE LEGEND OF SLEEPY HOLLOW
by Washington Irving
Ichabod Crane...
ODE TO
HEH.
...is kind of a wuss.
A HEADLESS HORSEMAN!
AAAAH!

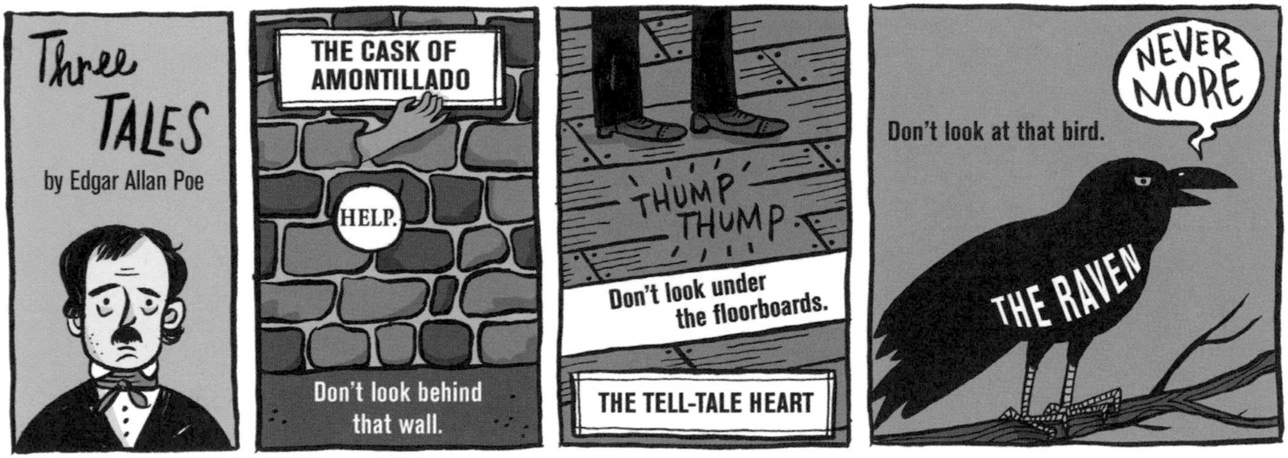
Three TALES
by Edgar Allan Poe
THE CASK OF AMONTILLADO
HELP.
Don't look behind that wall.
THUMP THUMP
Don't look under the floorboards.
THE TELL-TALE HEART
Don't look at that bird.
NEVER MORE
THE RAVEN

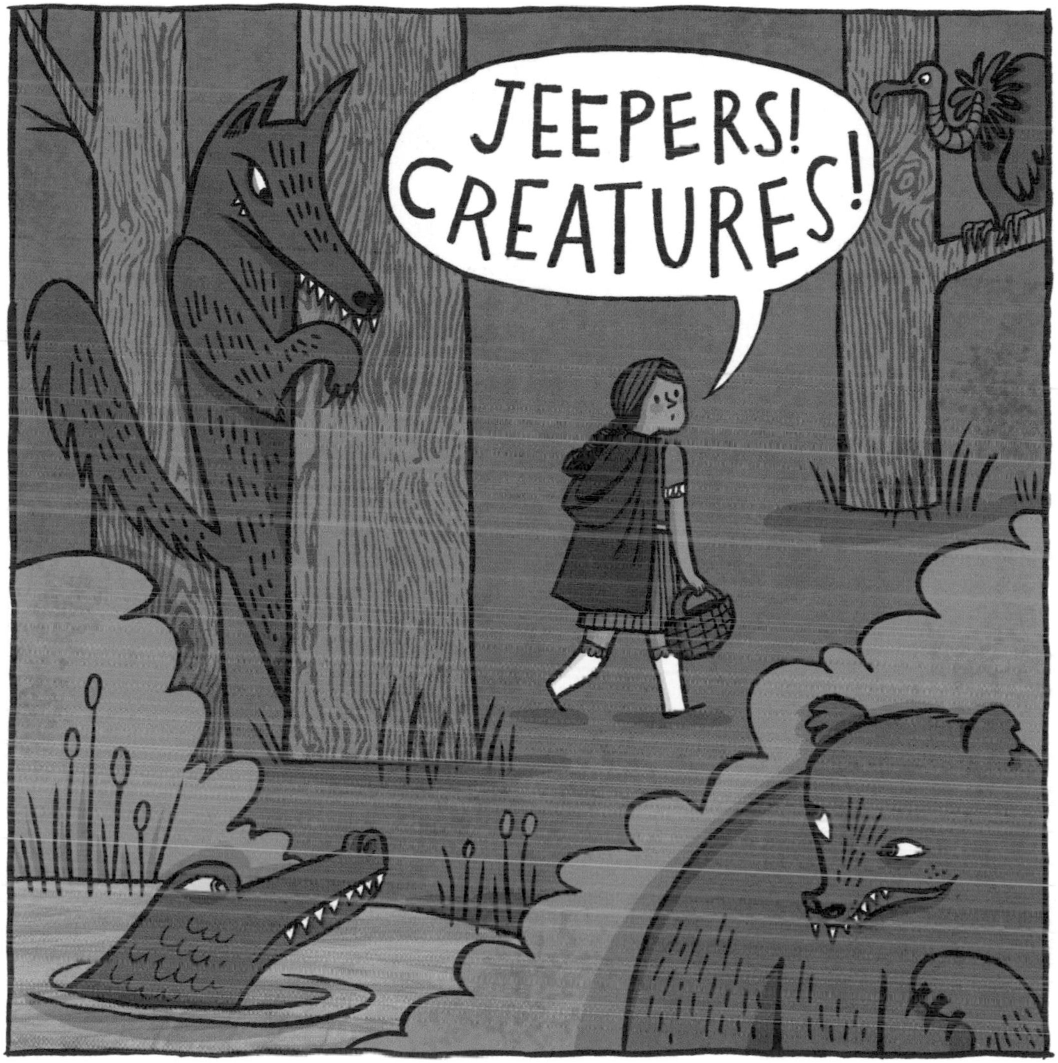
JEEPERS! CREATURES!

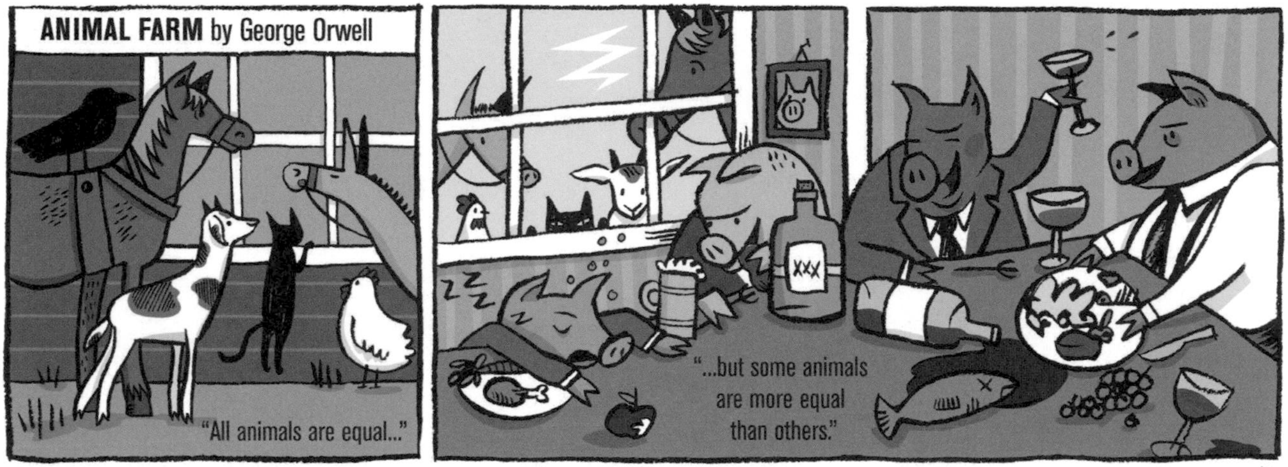
ANIMAL FARM by George Orwell
"All animals are equal..."
XXX
"...but some animals are more equal than others."

SEE "THOUGHTS"

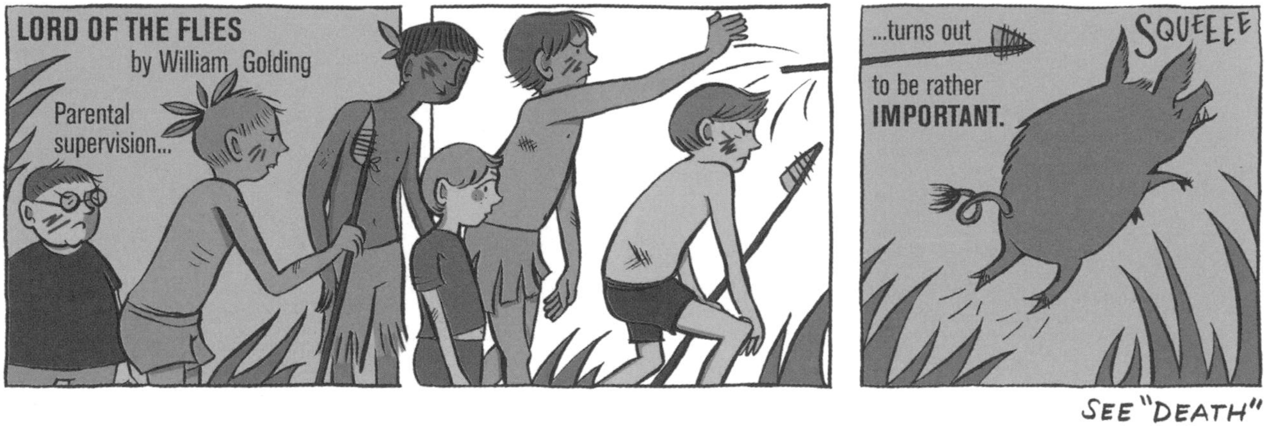
LORD OF THE FLIES by William Golding
Parental supervision...
...turns out to be rather IMPORTANT.
SQUEEEE

SEE "DEATH"

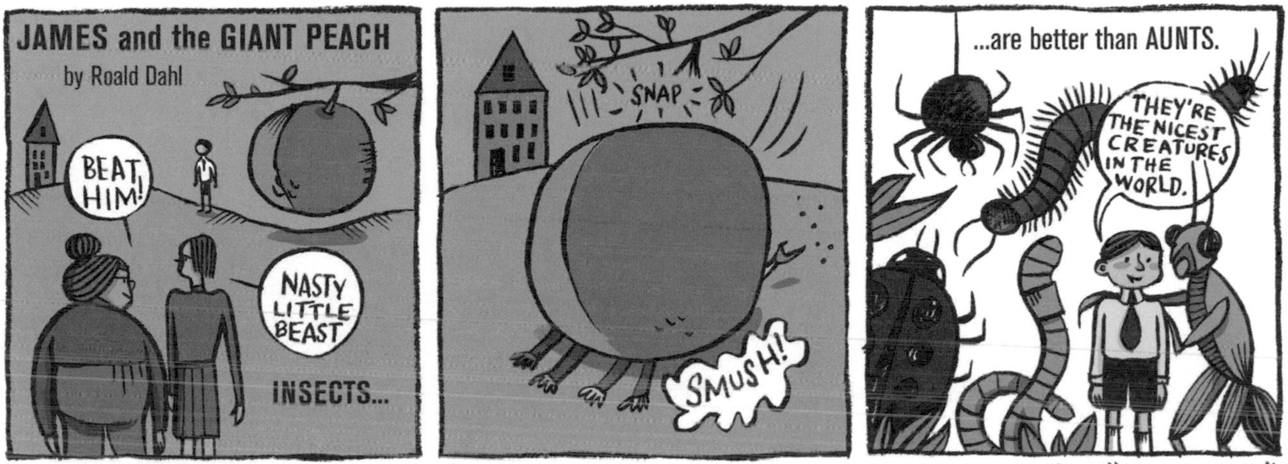
JAMES and the GIANT PEACH
by Roald Dahl
BEAT HIM!
NASTY LITTLE BEAST
INSECTS...
SNAP
SMUSH!
...are better than AUNTS.
THEY'RE THE NICEST CREATURES IN THE WORLD.

SEE "FAMILIES"

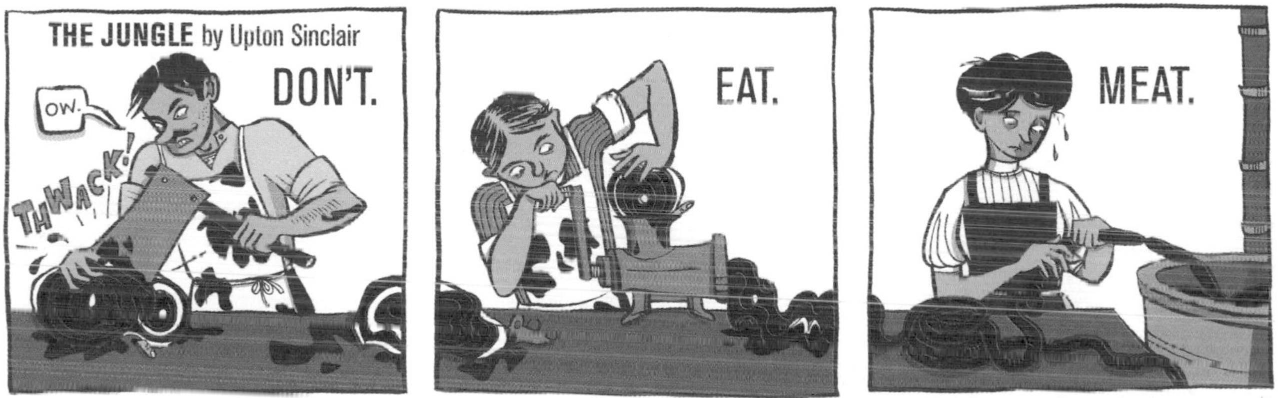
THE JUNGLE by Upton Sinclair
DON'T.
OW.
THWACK!
EAT.
MEAT.

SEE "HORROR"

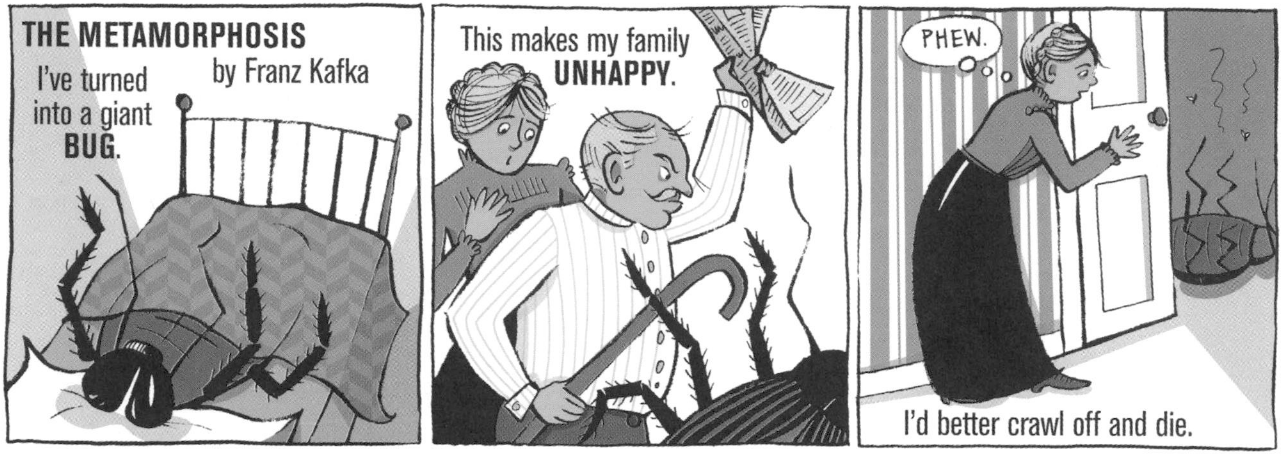
THE METAMORPHOSIS
by Franz Kafka
I've turned into a giant BUG.
This makes my family UNHAPPY.
PHEW.
I'd better crawl off and die.

SEE "FAMILIES"

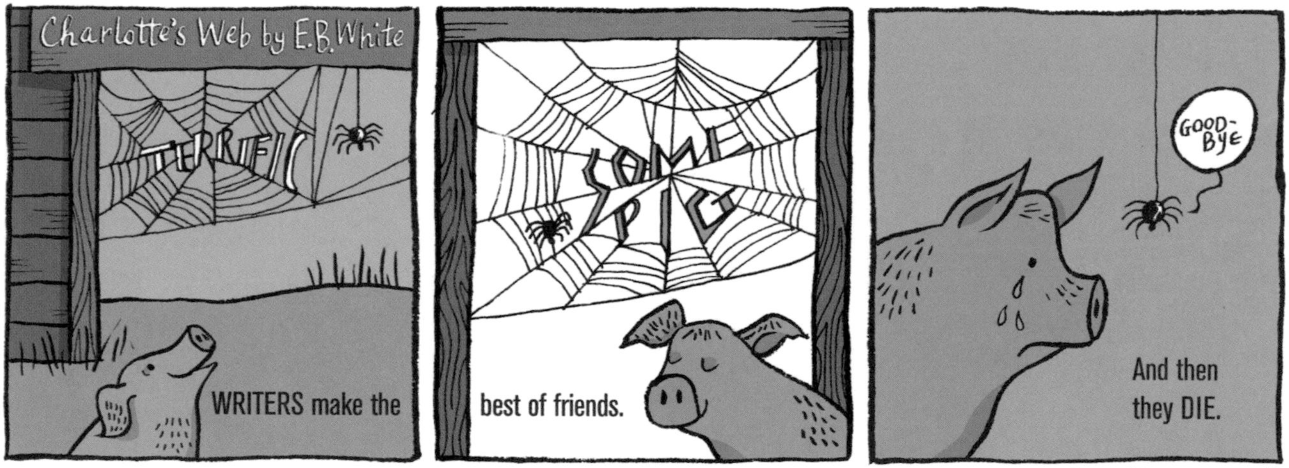
Charlotte's Web by E.B. White
TERRIFIC
WRITERS make the
SOME PIG
best of friends.
GOOD-BYE
And then they DIE.

SEE "FRIENDS"

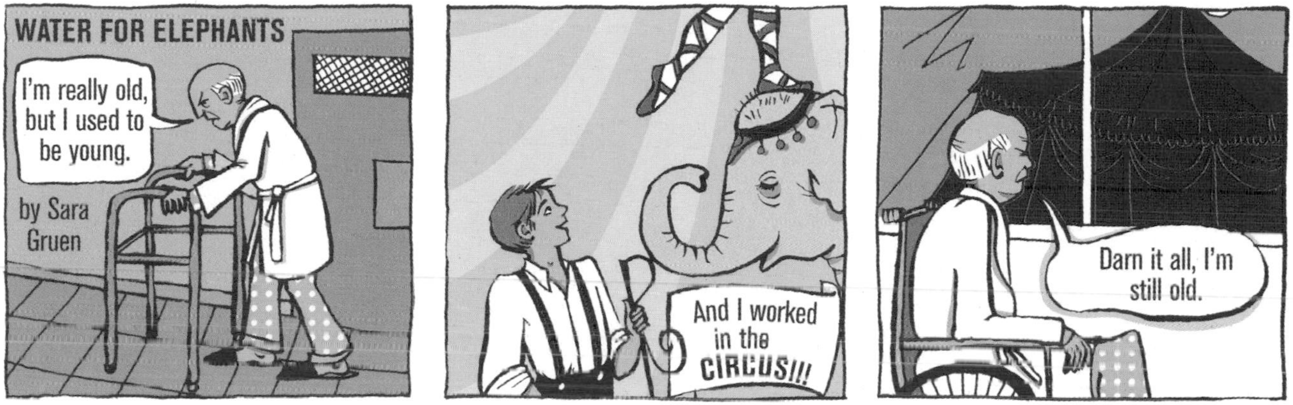
WATER FOR ELEPHANTS
I'm really old, but I used to be young.
by Sara Gruen
And I worked in the CIRCUS!!!
Darn it all, I'm still old.

SEE "EPIC"

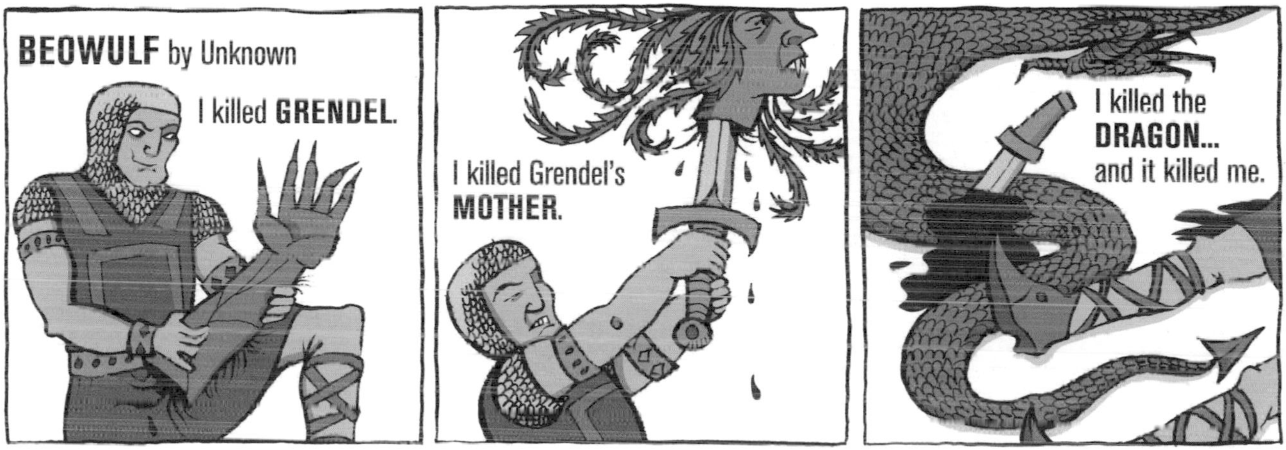
BEOWULF by Unknown
I killed GRENDEL.
I killed Grendel's MOTHER.
I killed the DRAGON... and it killed me.

SEE "DEATH"

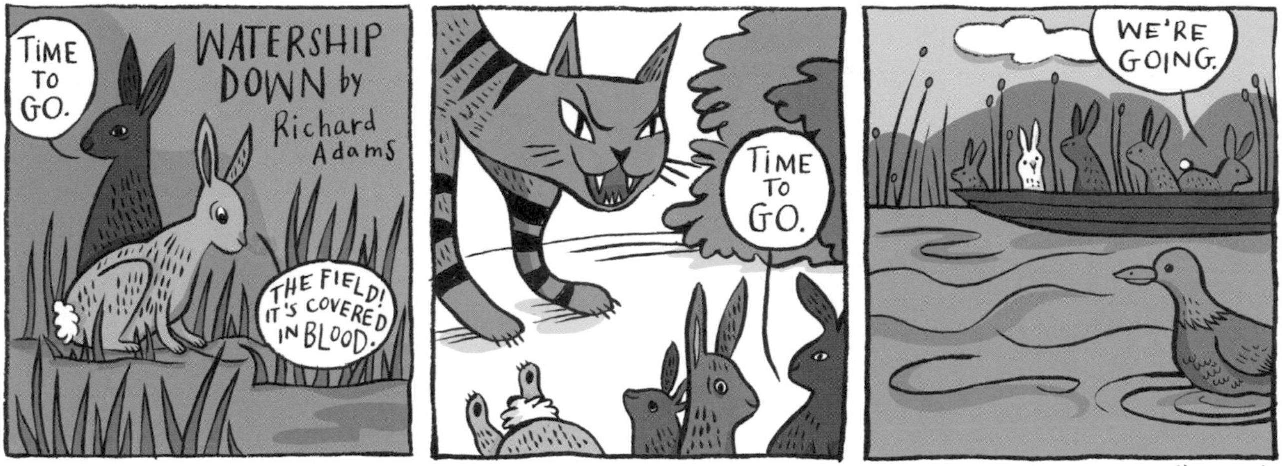
TIME TO GO.
WATERSHIP DOWN by Richard Adams
THE FIELD! IT'S COVERED IN BLOOD.
TIME TO GO.
WE'RE GOING.

SEE "EPIC"

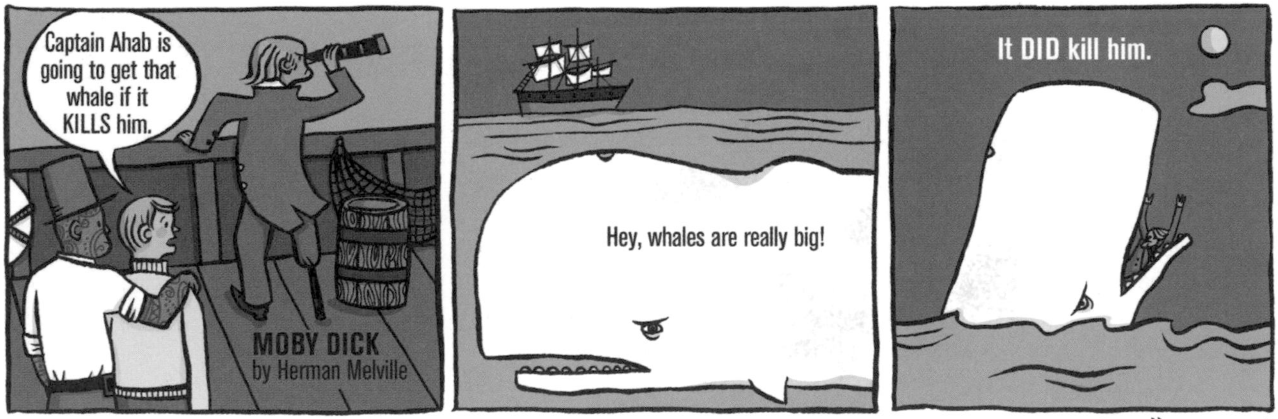
Captain Ahab is going to get that whale if it KILLS him.
MOBY DICK by Herman Melville
Hey, whales are really big!
It DID kill him.

SEE "DEATH"

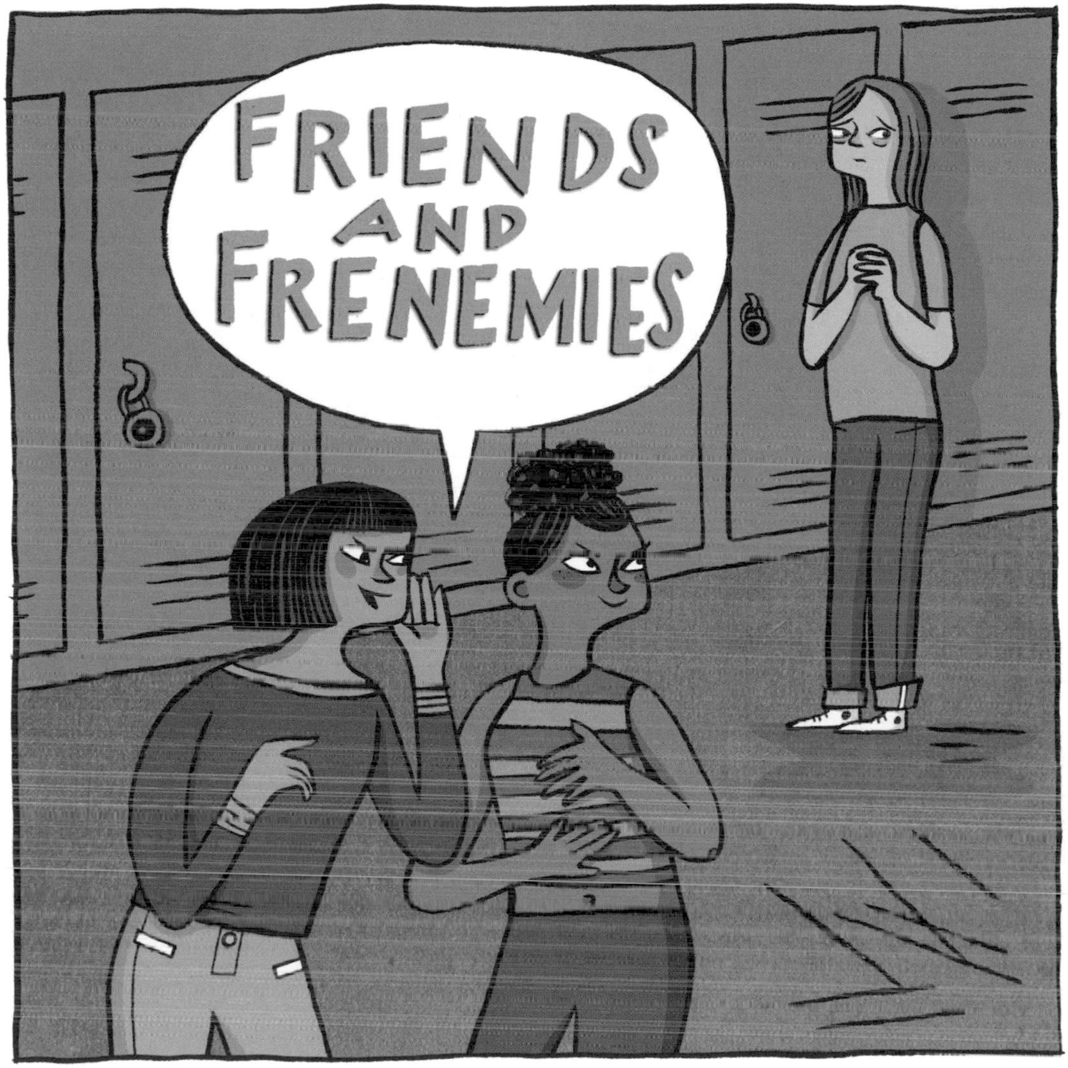
FRIENDS AND FRENEMIES

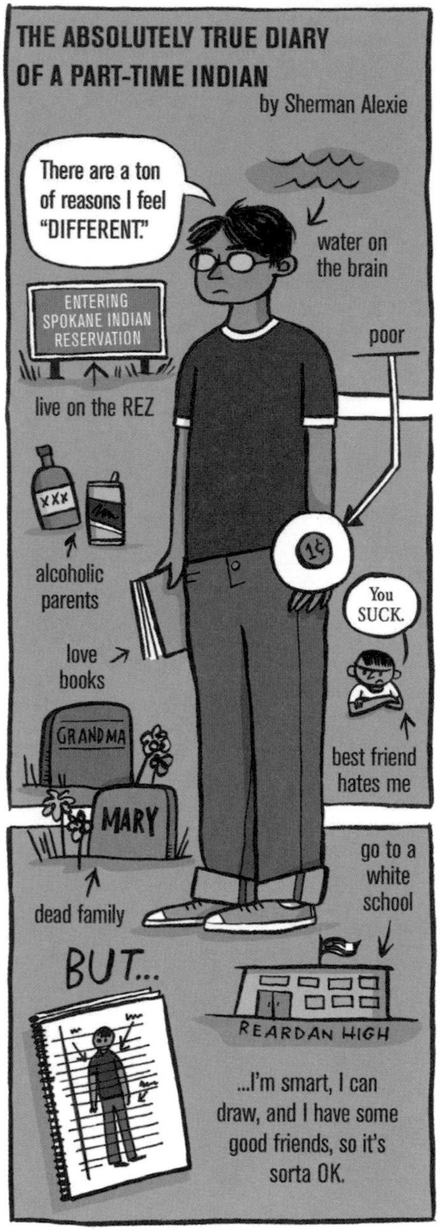
THE ABSOLUTELY TRUE DIARY OF A PART-TIME INDIAN
by Sherman Alexie
There are a ton of reasons I feel "DIFFERENT."
water on the brain
ENTERING SPOKANE INDIAN RESERVATION
live on the REZ
poor
1¢
XXX
alcoholic parents
love books
You SUCK.
best friend hates me
GRANDMA
MARY
dead family
go to a white school
BUT...
REARDAN HIGH
...I'm smart, I can draw, and I have some good friends, so it's sorta OK.

SEE "FAMILIES"

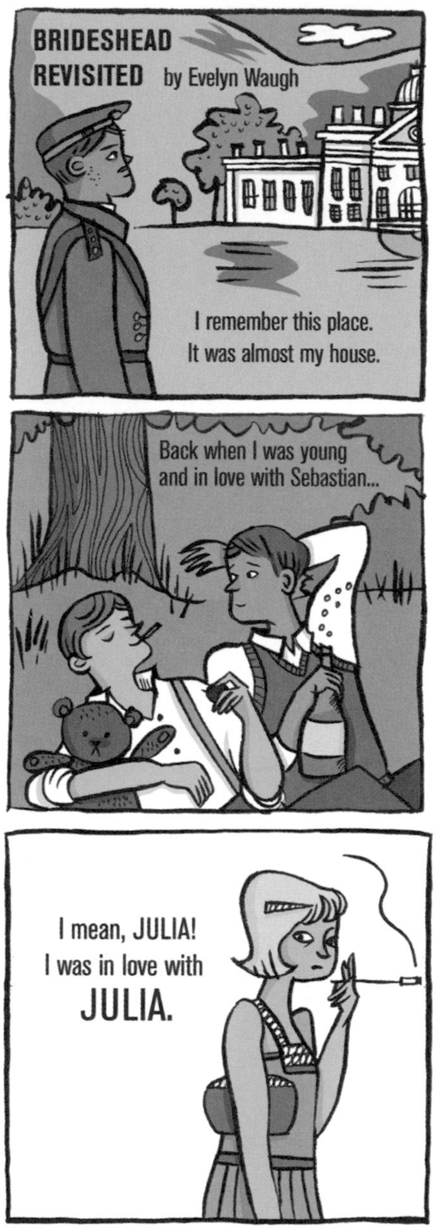
BRIDESHEAD REVISITED by Evelyn Waugh
I remember this place. It was almost my house.
Back when I was young and in love with Sebastian...
I mean, JULIA! I was in love with JULIA.

SEE "FAMILIES"

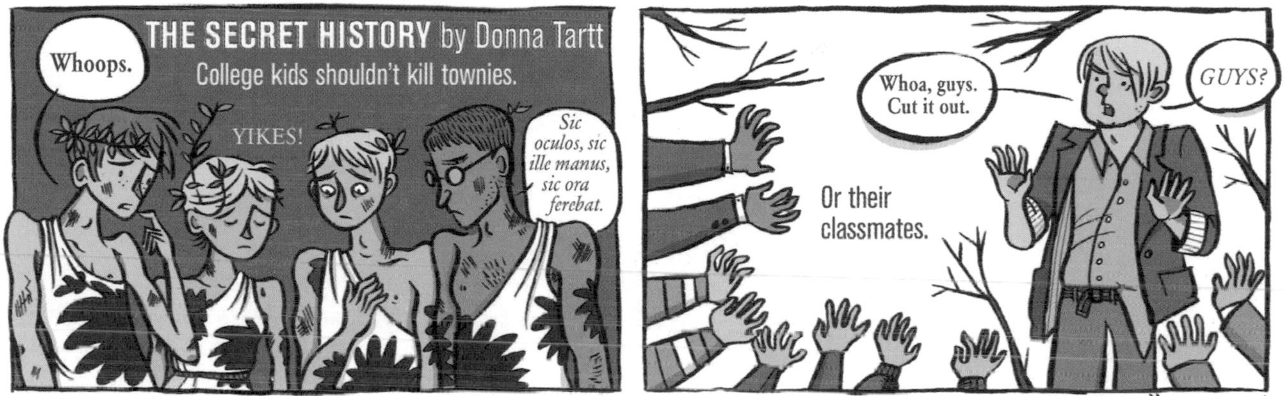
THE SECRET HISTORY by Donna Tartt
College kids shouldn't kill townies.
Whoops.
YIKES!
Sic oculos, sic ille manus, sic ora ferebat.
Or their classmates.
Whoa, guys. Cut it out.
GUYS?

SEE "DEATH"

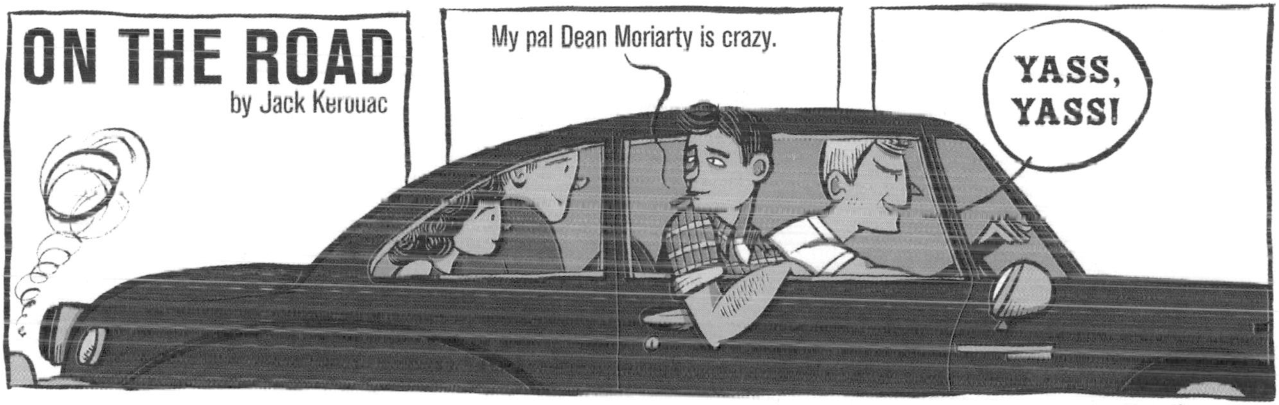
ON THE ROAD
by Jack Kerouac
My pal Dean Moriarty is crazy.
YASS, YASS!

SEE "EPIC"

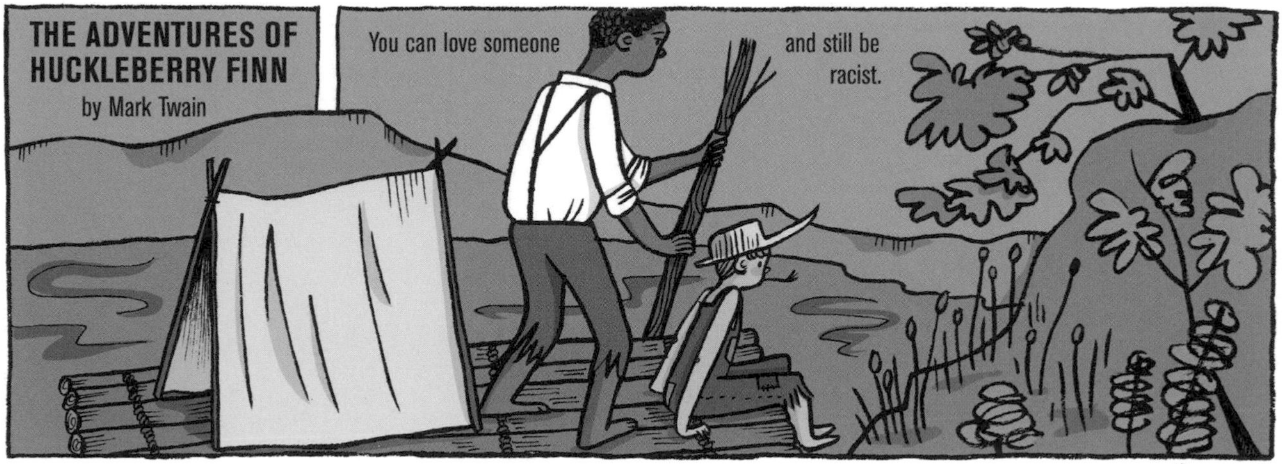
THE ADVENTURES OF HUCKLEBERRY FINN
by Mark Twain
You can love someone
and still be racist.

SEE "EPIC"

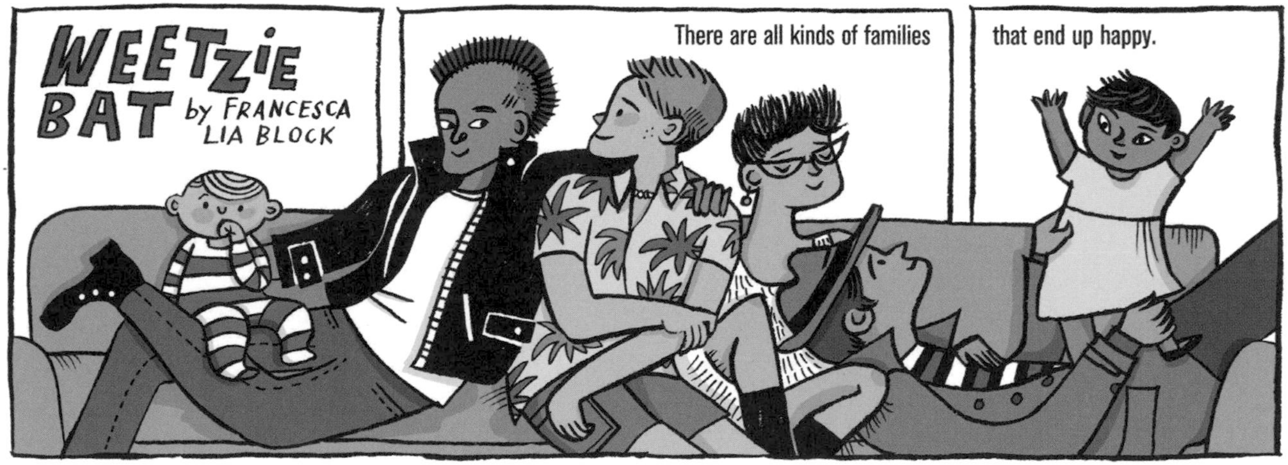
WEETZIE BAT by FRANCESCA LIA BLOCK
There are all kinds of families
that end up happy.

SEE "FAMILIES"

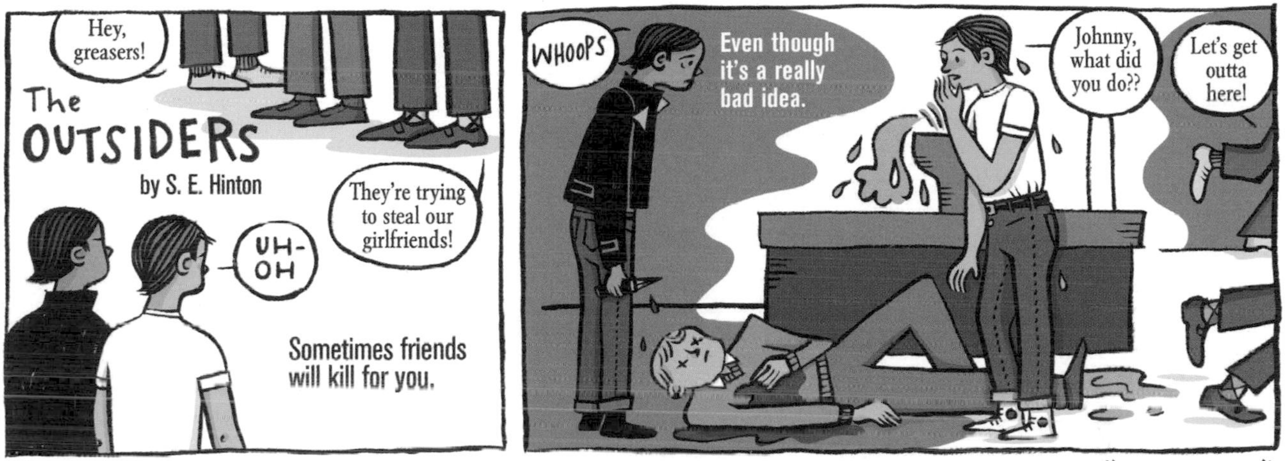
Hey, greasers!
The OUTSIDERS
by S. E. Hinton
They're trying to steal our girlfriends!
UH-OH
Sometimes friends will kill for you.
WHOOPS
Even though it's a really bad idea.
Johnny, what did you do??
Let's get outta here!

SEE "FAMILIES"

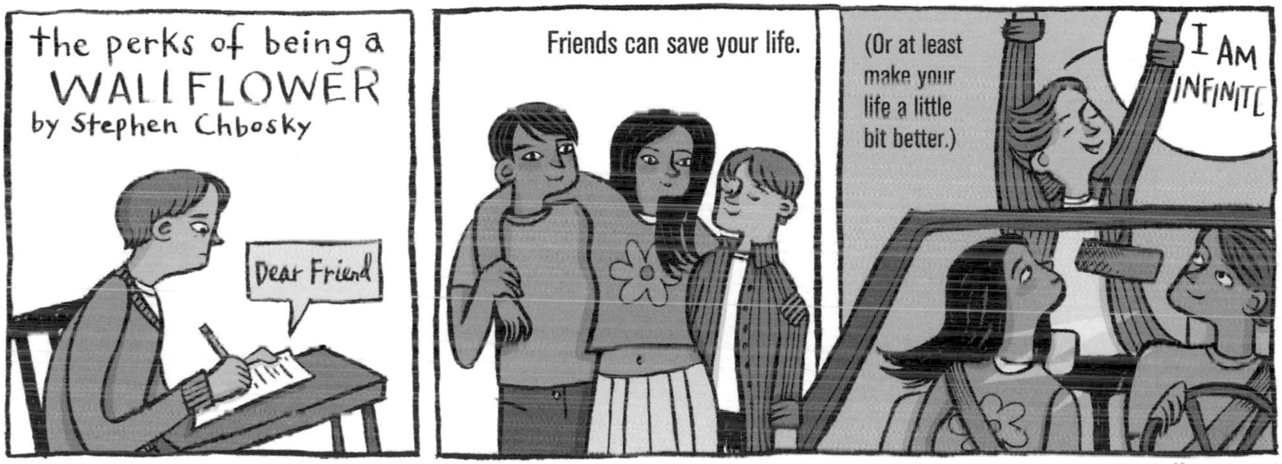
the perks of being a WALLFLOWER
by Stephen Chbosky
Dear Friend
Friends can save your life.
(Or at least make your life a little bit better.)
I AM INFINITE

SEE "LOVE"

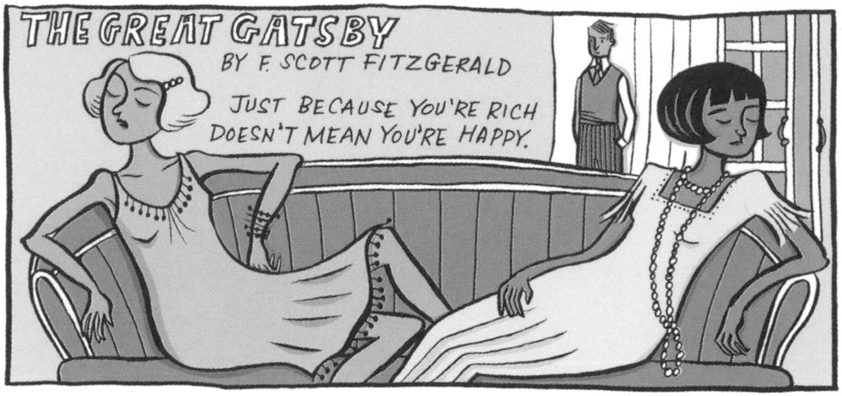
THE GREAT GATSBY
BY F. SCOTT FITZGERALD
JUST BECAUSE YOU'RE RICH DOESN'T MEAN YOU'RE HAPPY.

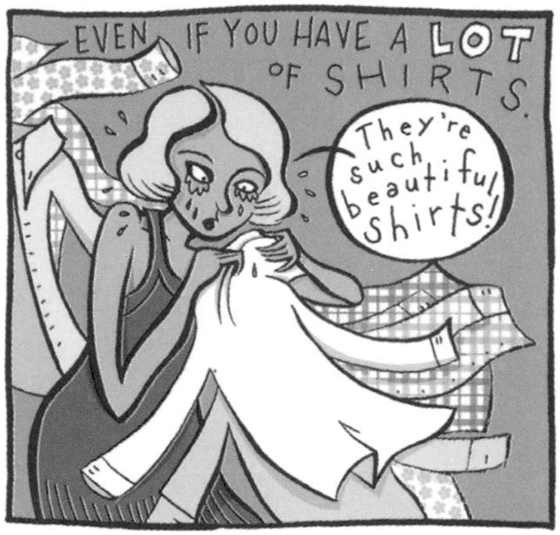
EVEN IF YOU HAVE A LOT OF SHIRTS.
They're such beautiful shirts!

SEE "LOVE"

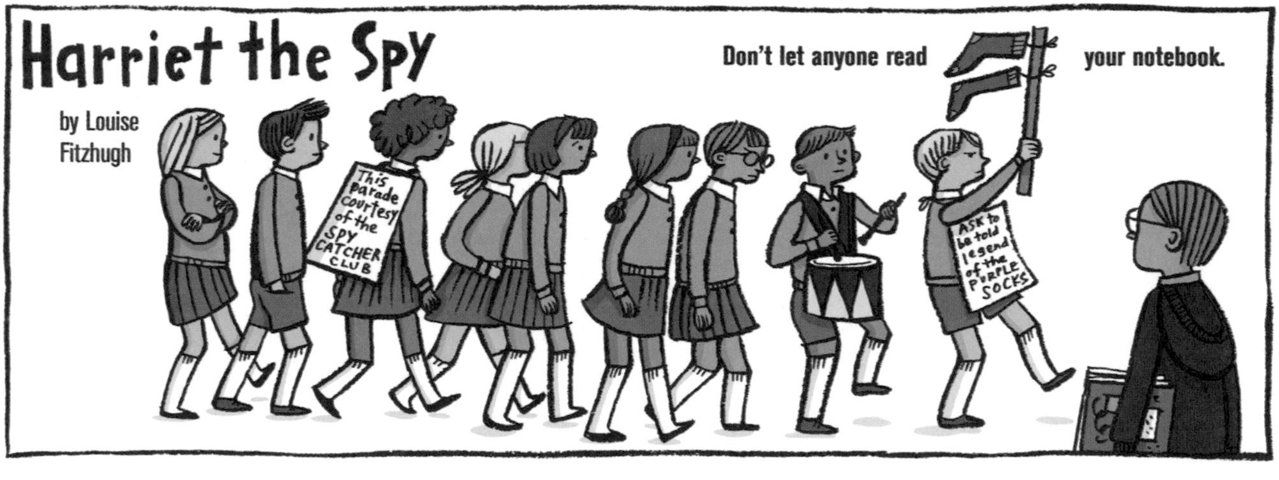
Harriet the Spy
by Louise Fitzhugh
Don't let anyone read your notebook.
This parade courtesy of the SPY CATCHER CLUB
ASK to be told legend of the PURPLE SOCKS

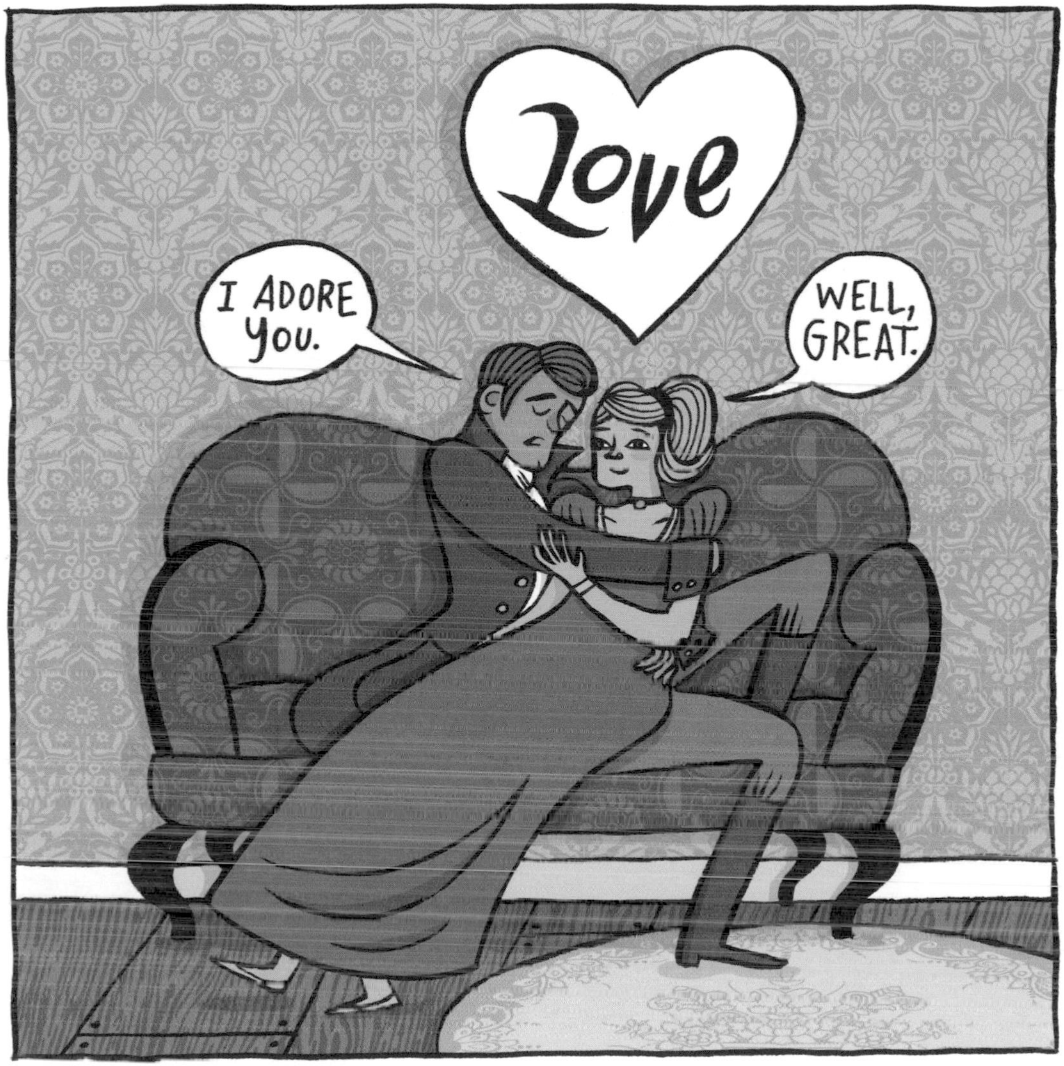
Love
I ADORE YOU.
WELL, GREAT.

HOW to READ PROUST in the ORIGINAL

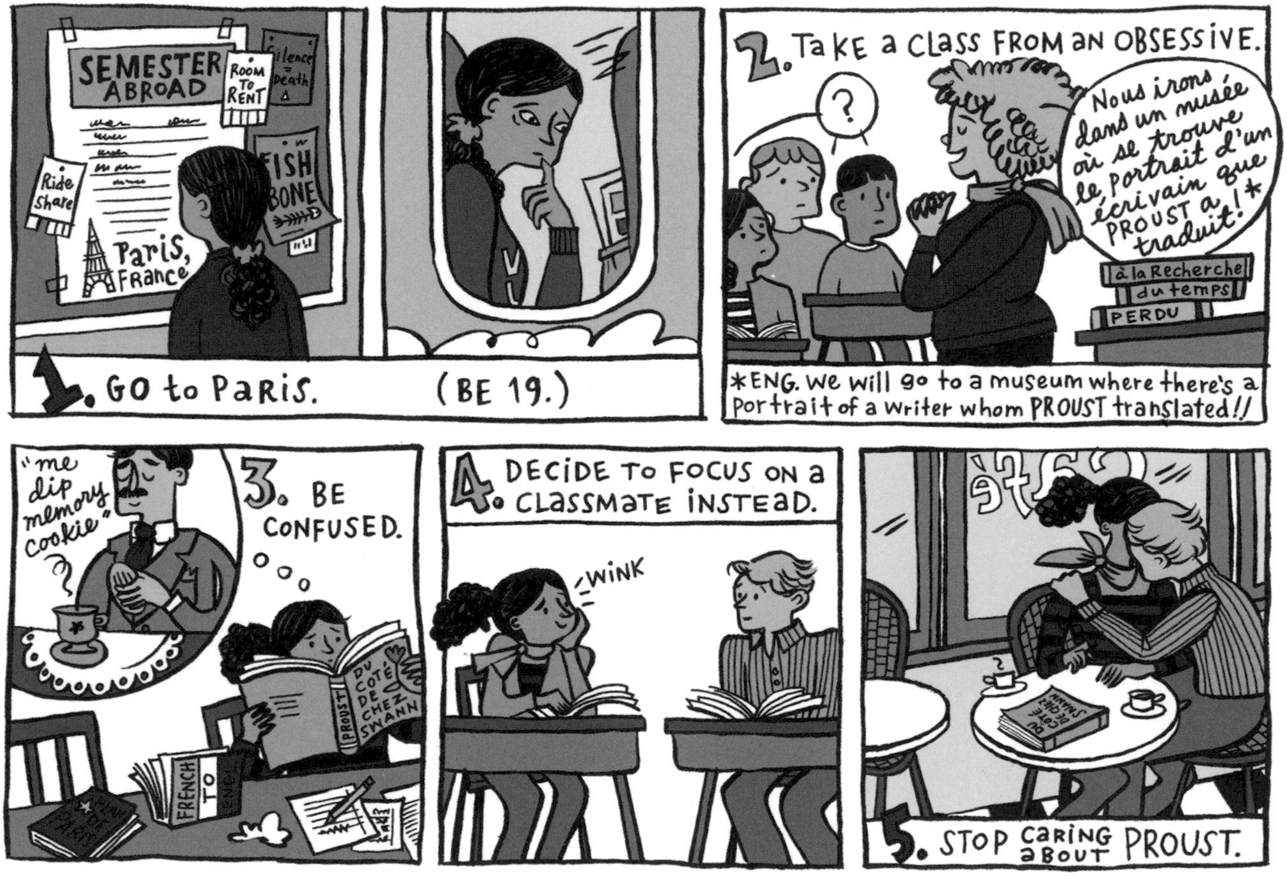
SEMESTER ABROAD
ROOM TO RENT
Silence = Death
Ride Share
FISH BONE
Paris, France
1. GO to PaRiS.
(BE 19.)
2. TaKE a CLaSS FROM aN OBSESSiVE.
?
Nous irons dans un musée où se trouve le portrait d'un écrivain que PROUST a traduit!*
à la Recherche
du temps
PERDU
*ENG. We will go to a museum where there's a portrait of a writer whom PROUST translated!!
"me dip memory cookie"
3. BE CONFUSED.
DU COTÉ DE CHEZ SWANN
PROUST
FRENCH TO ENG.
PARIS
4. DECiDE TO FOCUS ON a CLaSSMaTE iNSTEaD.
WINK
DU COTÉ DE CHEZ SWANN
5. STOP CaRiNG aBOUT PROUST.

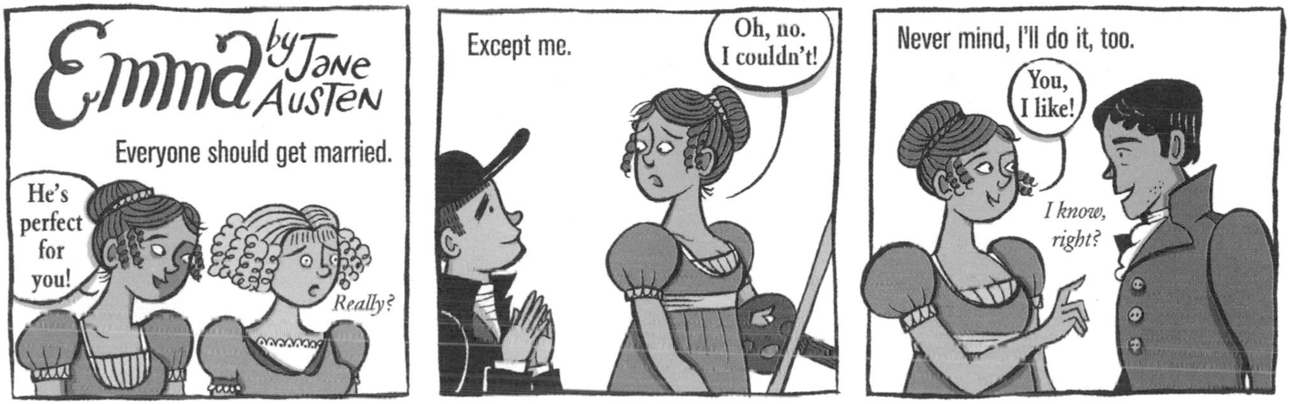
Emma by Jane Austen
Everyone should get married.
He's perfect for you!
Really?
Except me.
Oh, no. I couldn't!
Never mind, I'll do it, too.
You, I like!
I know, right?

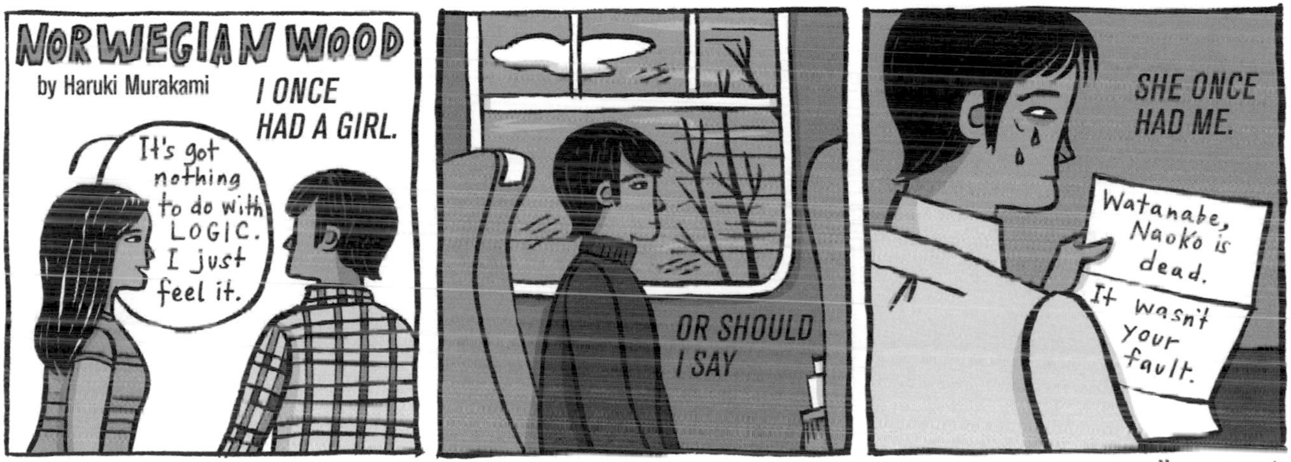
NORWEGIAN WOOD
by Haruki Murakami
I ONCE HAD A GIRL.
It's got nothing to do with LOGIC. I just feel it.
OR SHOULD I SAY
SHE ONCE HAD ME.
Watanabe, Naoko is dead.
It wasn't your fault.

SEE "DEATH"

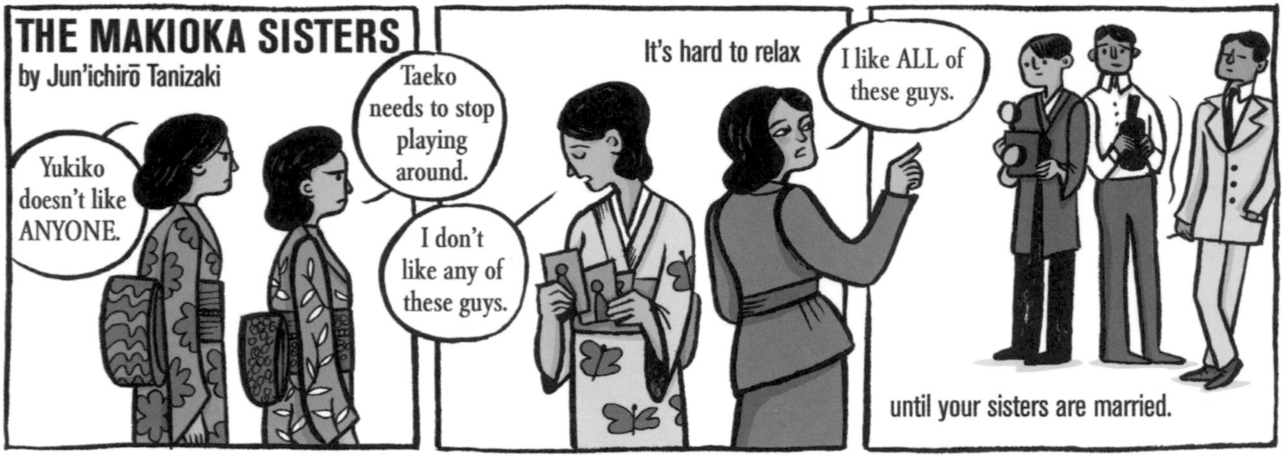
THE MAKIOKA SISTERS
by Jun'ichirō Tanizaki
Yukiko doesn't like ANYONE.
Taeko needs to stop playing around.
I don't like any of these guys.
It's hard to relax
I like ALL of these guys.
until your sisters are married.

SEE "FAMILIES"

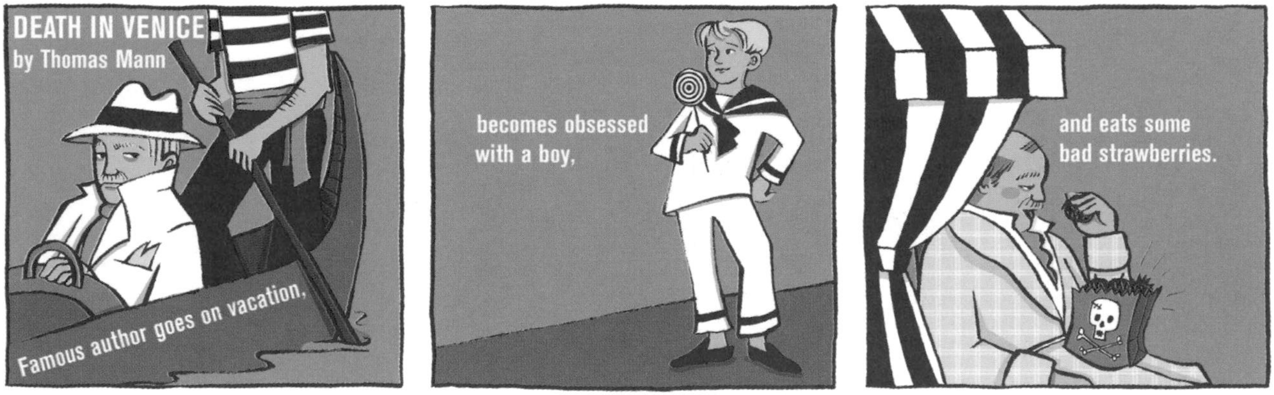
DEATH IN VENICE
by Thomas Mann
Famous author goes on vacation,
becomes obsessed with a boy,
and eats some bad strawberries.

SEE "DEATH"

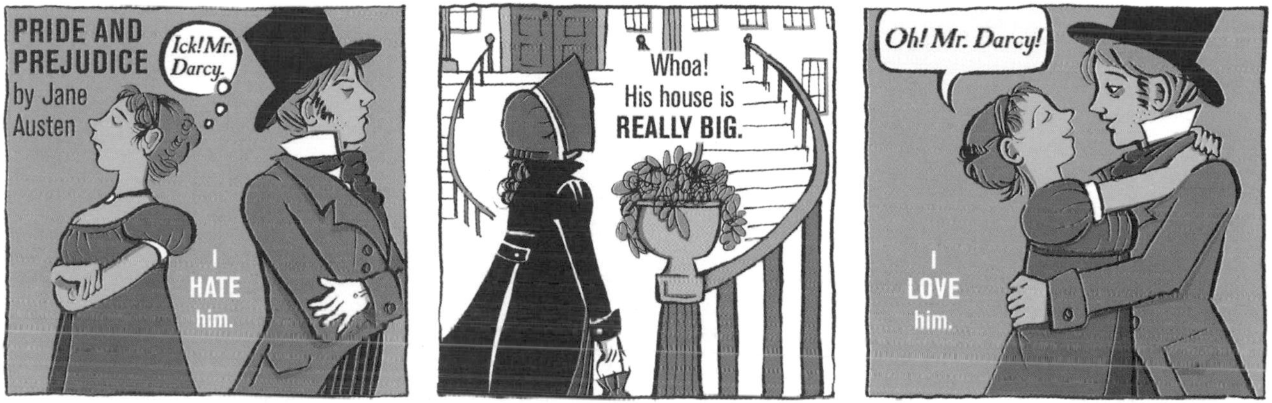
PRIDE AND PREJUDICE by Jane Austen
Ick! Mr. Darcy.
I HATE him.
Whoa! His house is REALLY BIG.
Oh! Mr. Darcy!
I LOVE him.

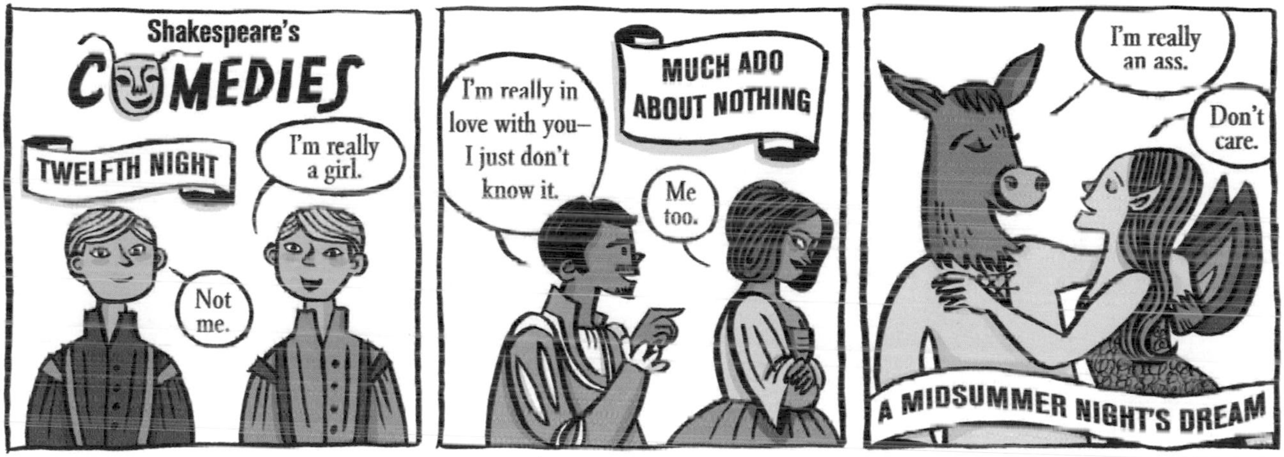
Shakespeare's COMEDIES
TWELFTH NIGHT
I'm really a girl.
Not me.
MUCH ADO ABOUT NOTHING
I'm really in love with you— I just don't know it.
Me too.
I'm really an ass.
Don't care.
A MIDSUMMER NIGHT'S DREAM

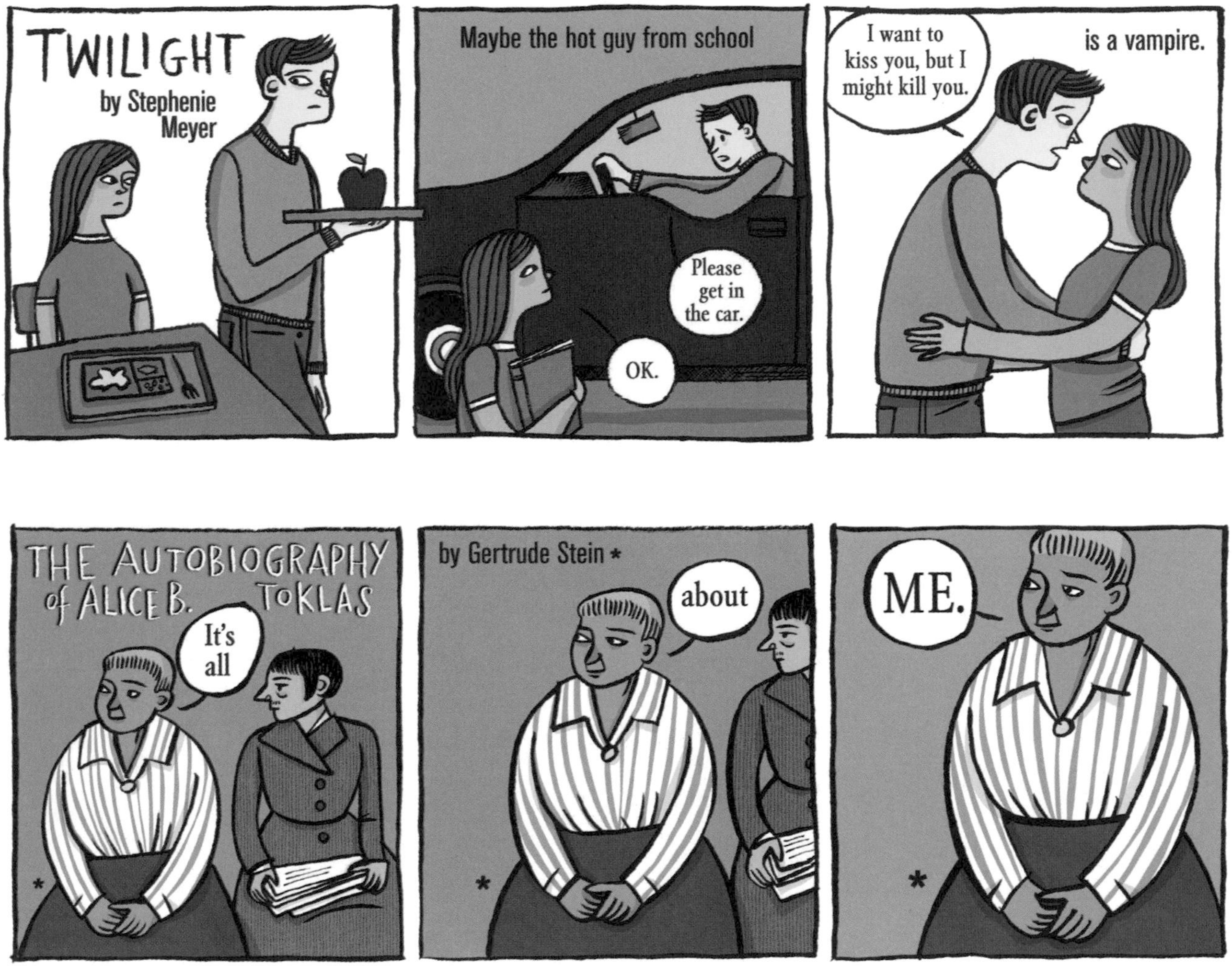
TWILIGHT
by Stephenie Meyer
Maybe the hot guy from school
Please get in the car.
OK.
I want to kiss you, but I might kill you.
is a vampire.
THE AUTOBIOGRAPHY of ALICE B. TOKLAS
It's all
by Gertrude Stein *
about
ME.

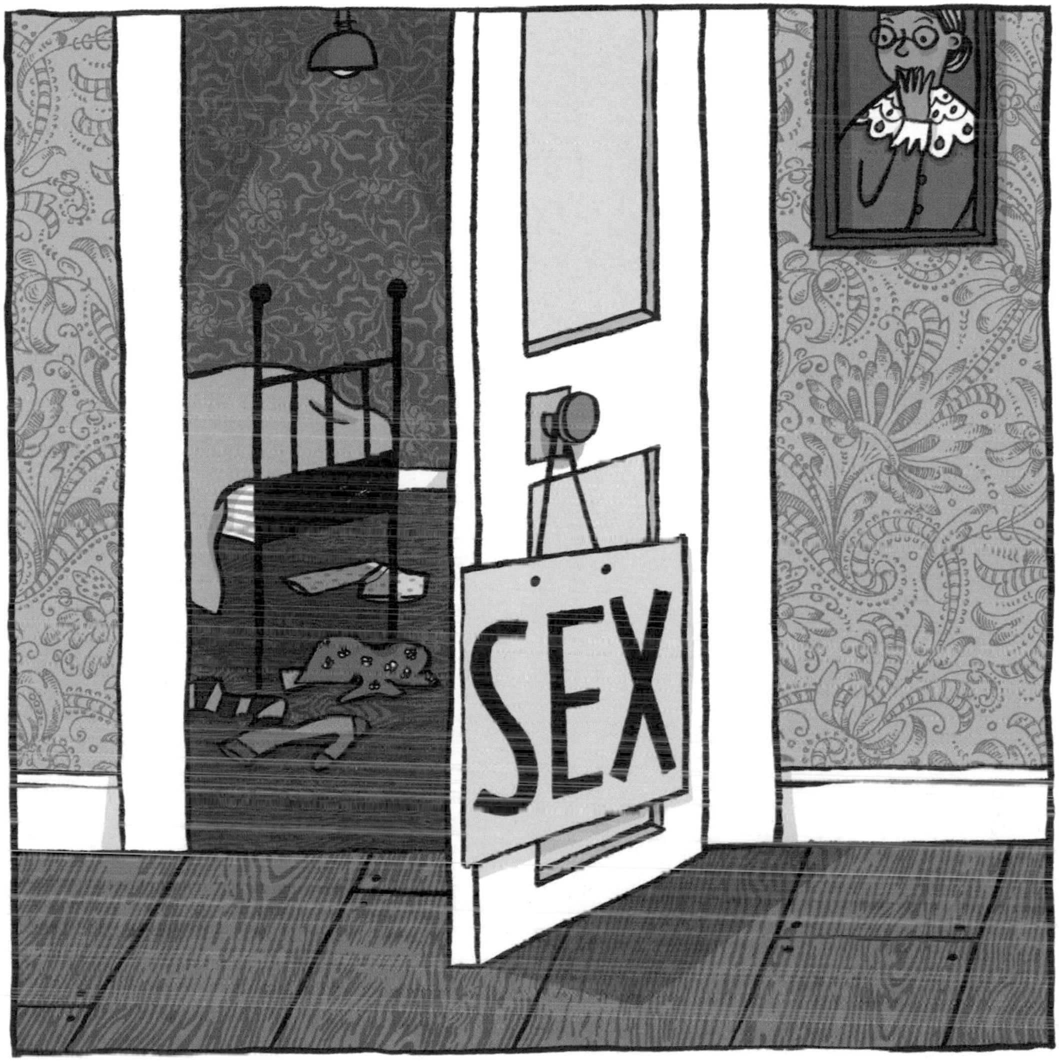
SEX

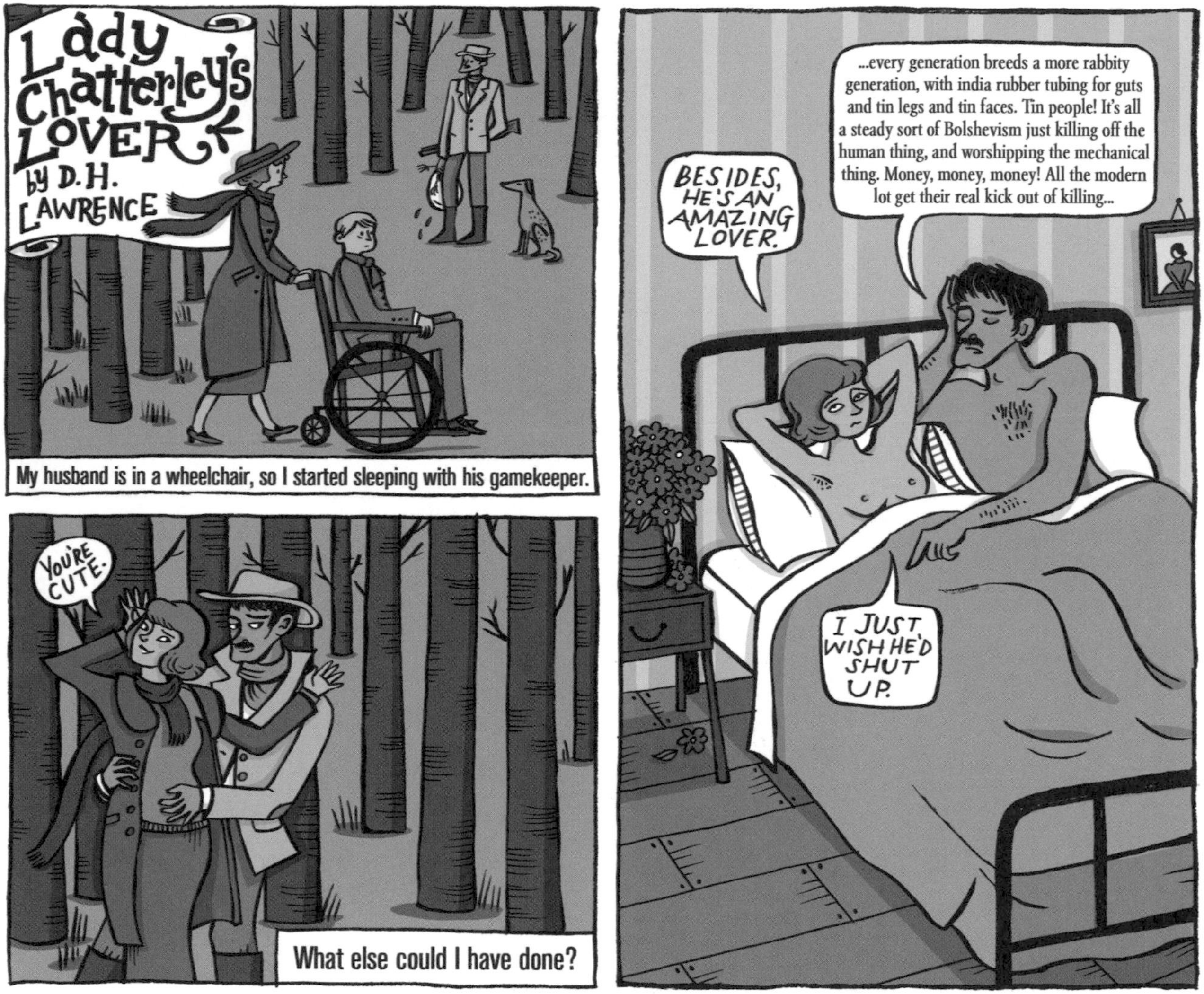

Lady Chatterley's LOVER by D.H. LAWRENCE
My husband is in a wheelchair, so I started sleeping with his gamekeeper.
YOU'RE CUTE.
What else could I have done?
...every generation breeds a more rabbity generation, with india rubber tubing for guts and tin legs and tin faces. Tin people! It's all a steady sort of Bolshevism just killing off the human thing, and worshipping the mechanical thing. Money, money, money! All the modern lot get their real kick out of killing...
BESIDES, HE'S AN AMAZING LOVER.
I JUST WISH HE'D SHUT UP.

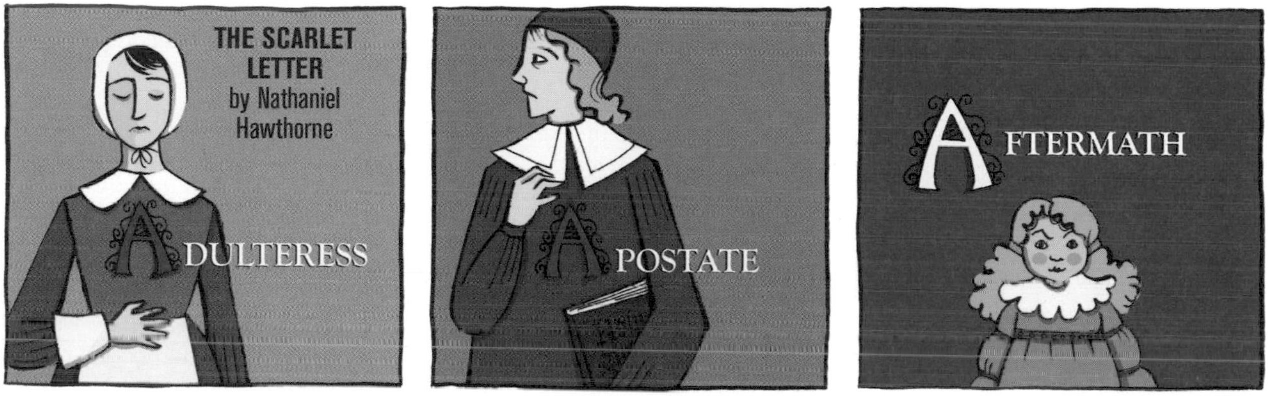
THE SCARLET LETTER
by Nathaniel Hawthorne
ADULTERESS
APOSTATE
AFTERMATH

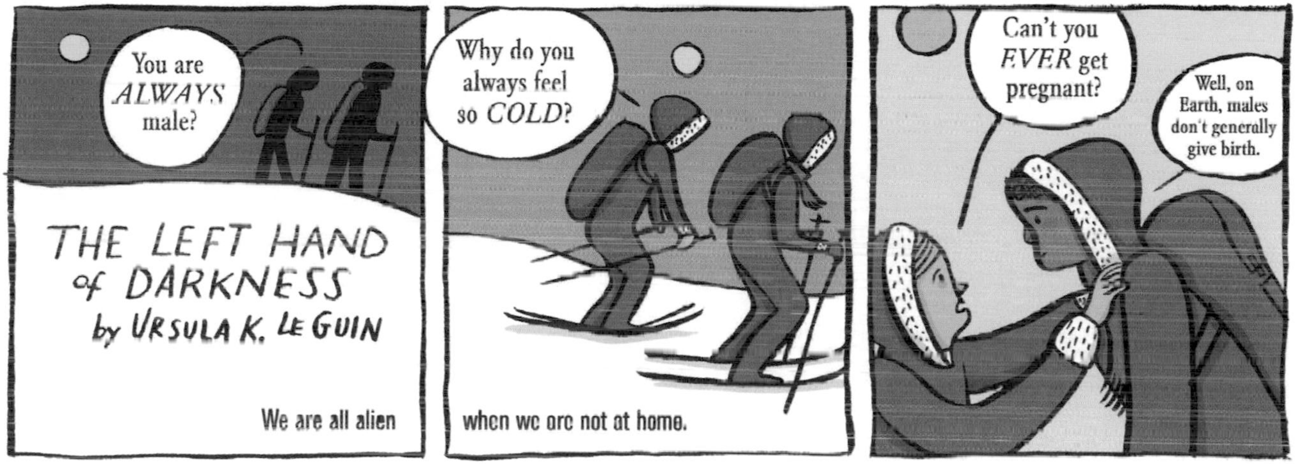
You are *ALWAYS* male?
THE LEFT HAND of DARKNESS
by URSULA K. LE GUIN
We are all alien
Why do you always feel so *COLD*?
when we are not at home.
Can't you *EVER* get pregnant?
Well, on Earth, males don't generally give birth.

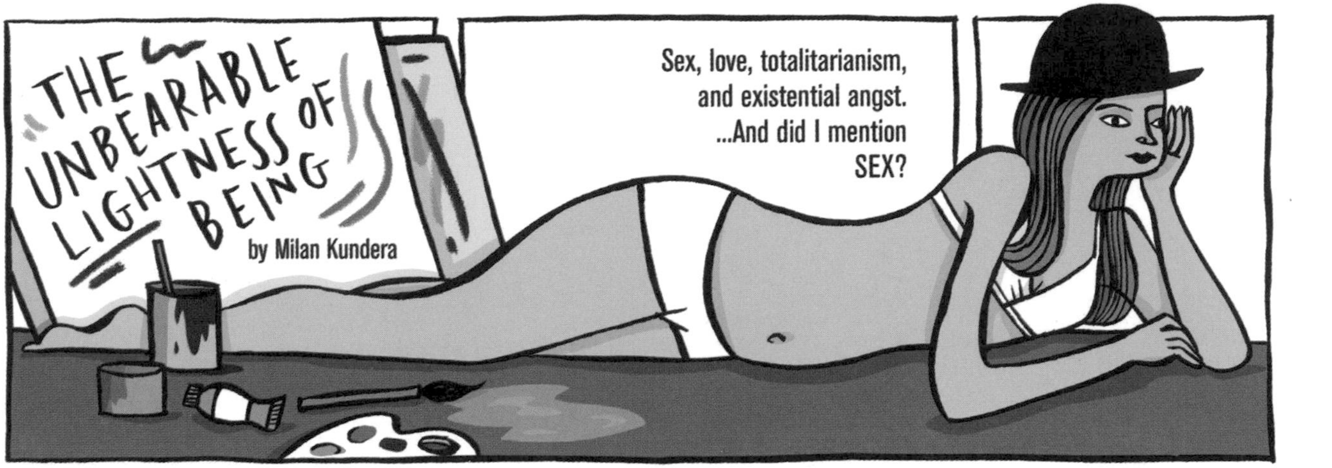
THE UNBEARABLE LIGHTNESS OF BEING
by Milan Kundera
Sex, love, totalitarianism, and existential angst. ...And did I mention SEX?

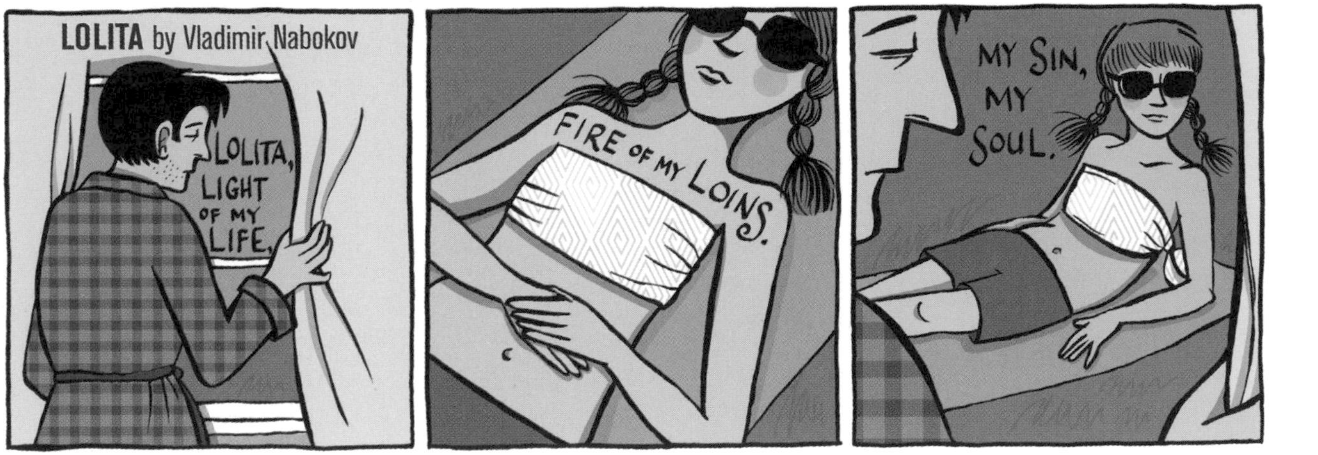
LOLITA by Vladimir Nabokov
LOLITA, LIGHT OF MY LIFE,
FIRE OF MY LOINS.
MY SIN, MY SOUL.

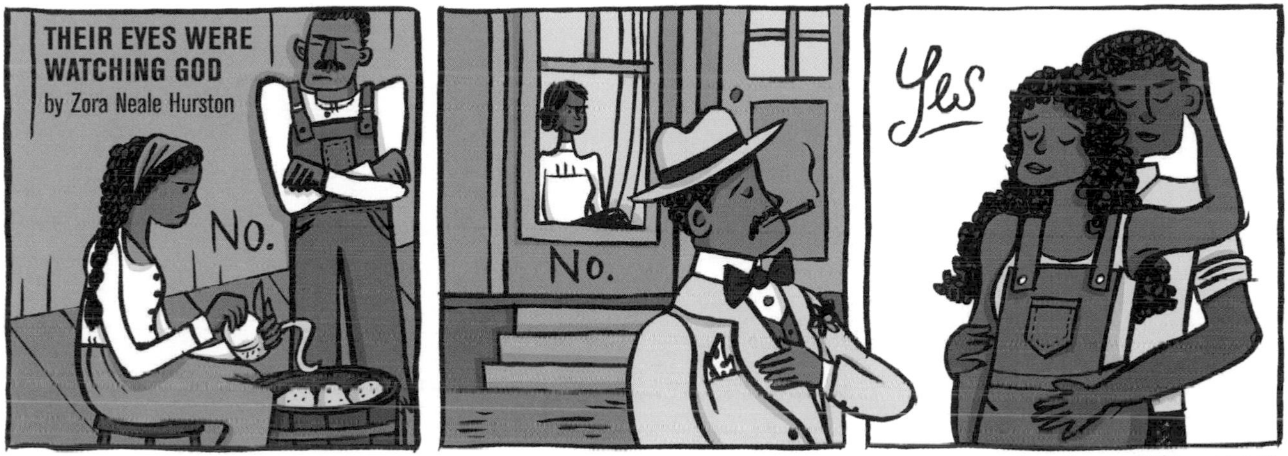
THEIR EYES WERE WATCHING GOD
by Zora Neale Hurston
No.
No.
Yes

SEE "LOVE," "DEATH"

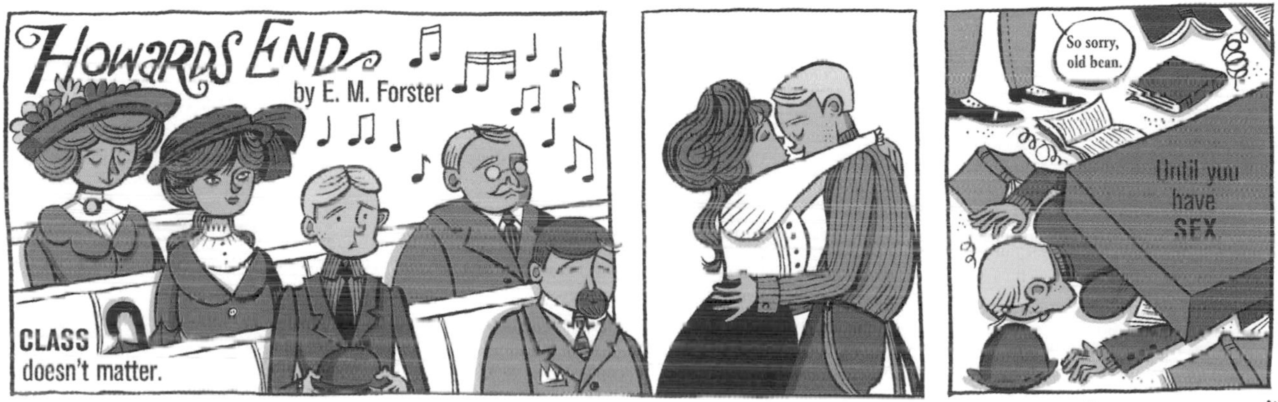
Howards End
by E. M. Forster
CLASS
doesn't matter.
So sorry, old bean.
Until you have SEX

SEE "THOUGHTS"

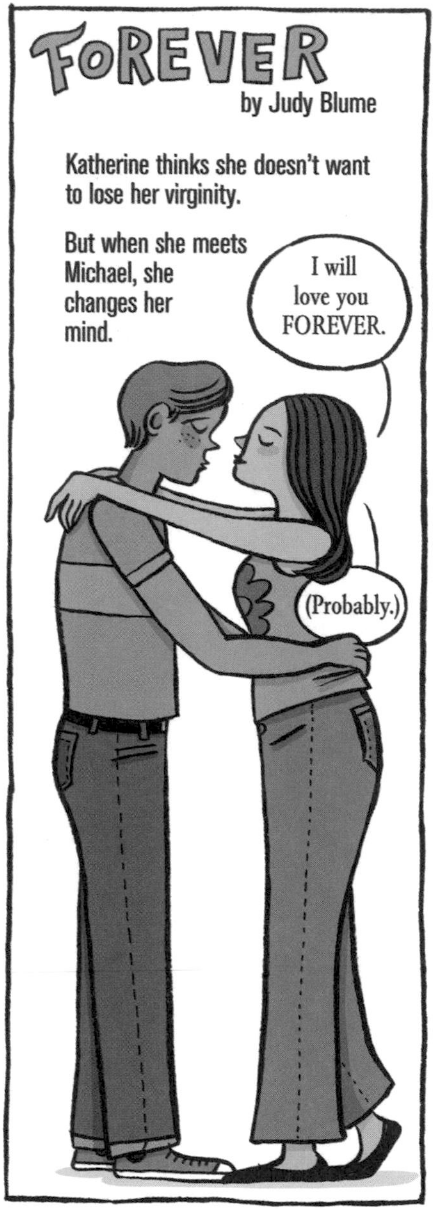
FOREVER
by Judy Blume
Katherine thinks she doesn't want to lose her virginity.
But when she meets Michael, she changes her mind.
I will love you FOREVER.
(Probably.)

SEE "LOVE"

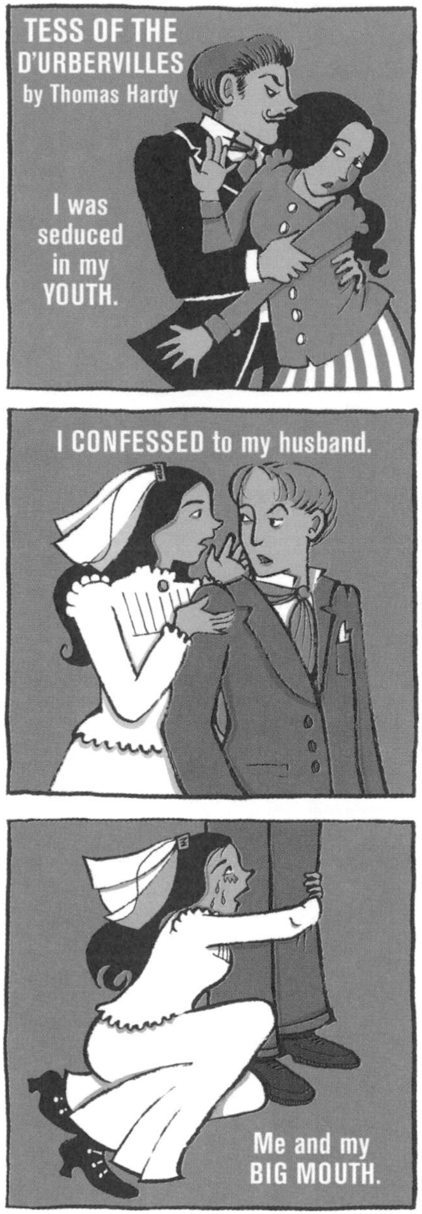
TESS OF THE D'URBERVILLES
by Thomas Hardy
I was seduced in my YOUTH.
I CONFESSED to my husband.
Me and my BIG MOUTH.

SEE "FEMALE"

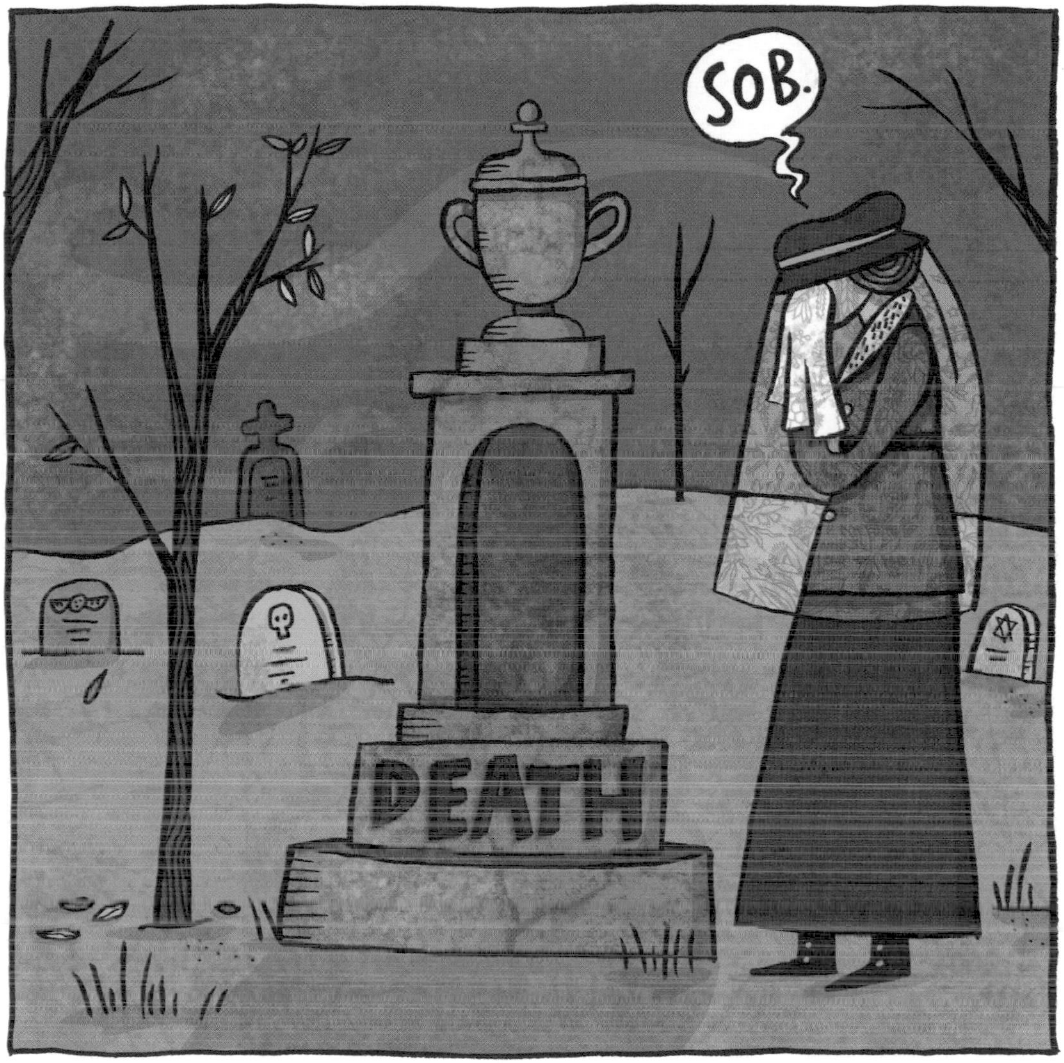
SOB.
DEATH

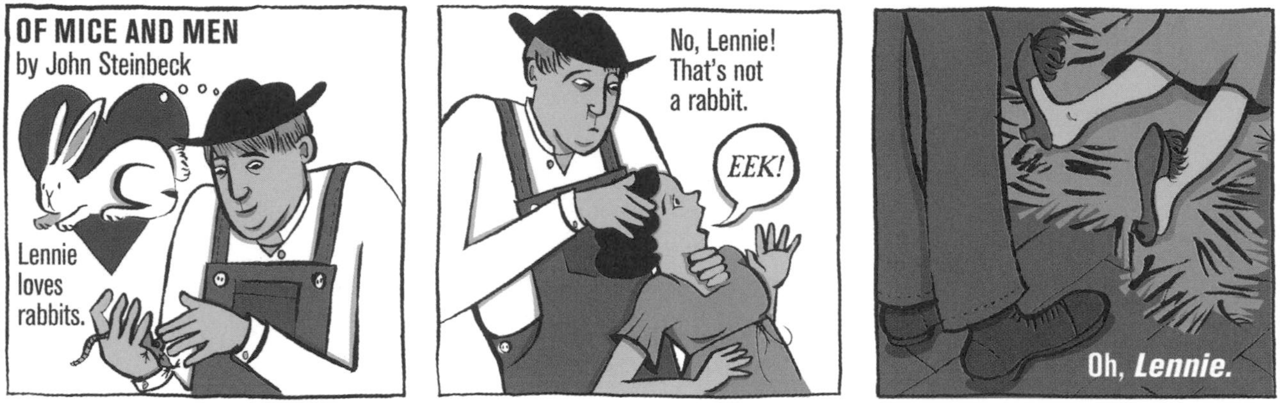
OF MICE AND MEN
by John Steinbeck
Lennie loves rabbits.
No, Lennie! That's not a rabbit.
EEK!
Oh, *Lennie.*

SEE "FEMALE"

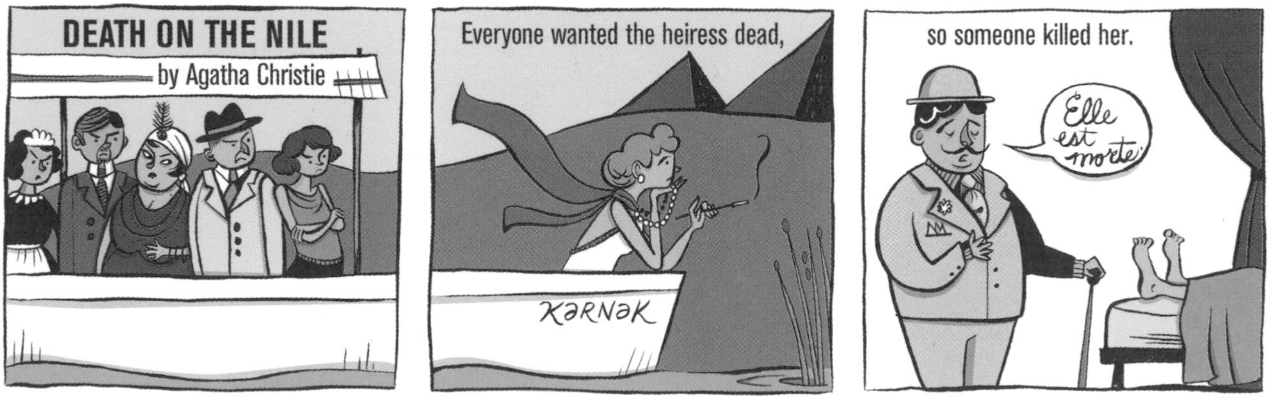
DEATH ON THE NILE
by Agatha Christie
Everyone wanted the heiress dead,
KARNAK
so someone killed her.
Elle est morte

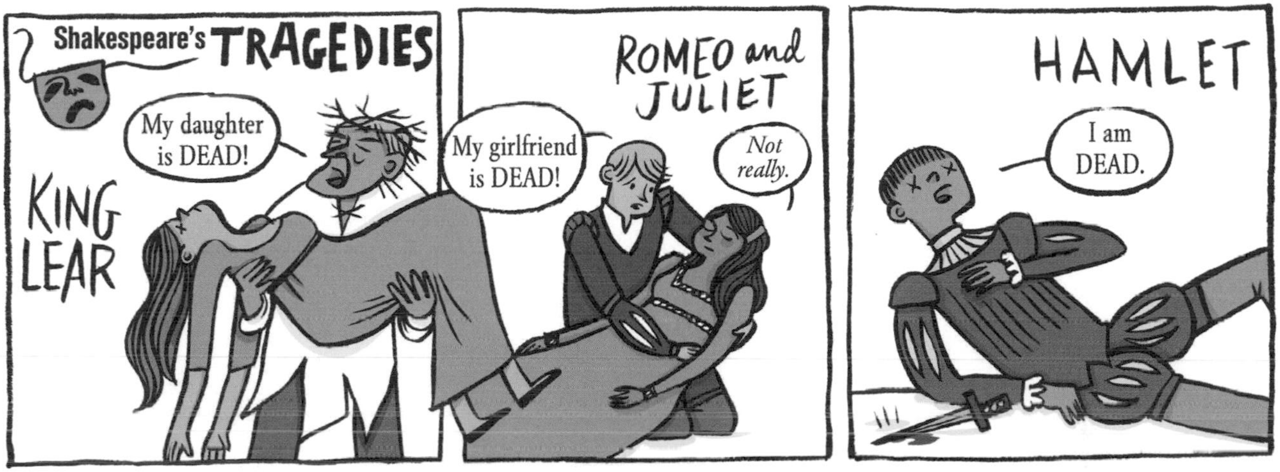
Shakespeare's TRAGEDIES
KING LEAR
My daughter is DEAD!
ROMEO and JULIET
My girlfriend is DEAD!
Not really.
HAMLET
I am DEAD.

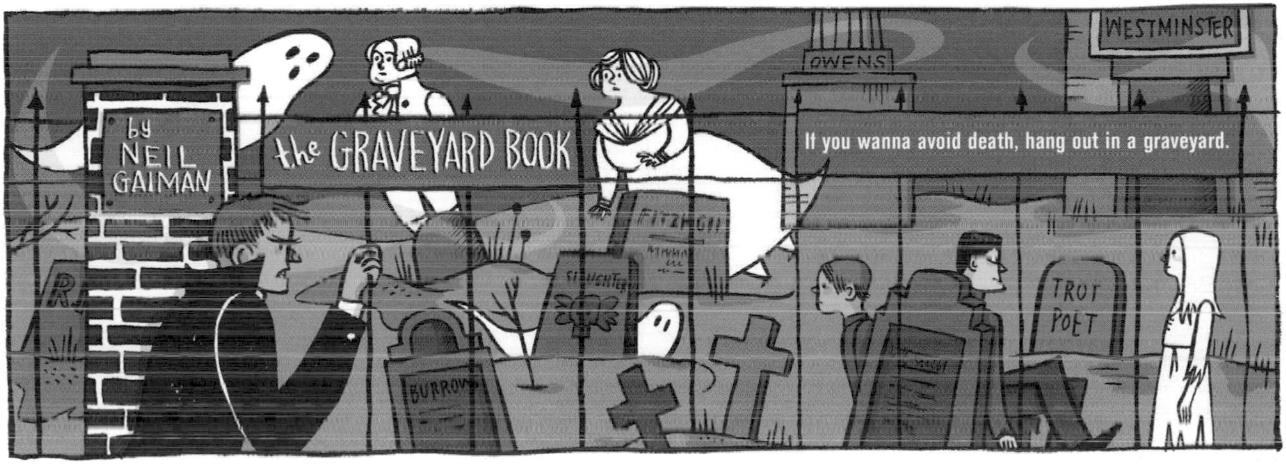
by NEIL GAIMAN
the GRAVEYARD BOOK
If you wanna avoid death, hang out in a graveyard.
OWENS
WESTMINSTER
TROT POET
BURROWS

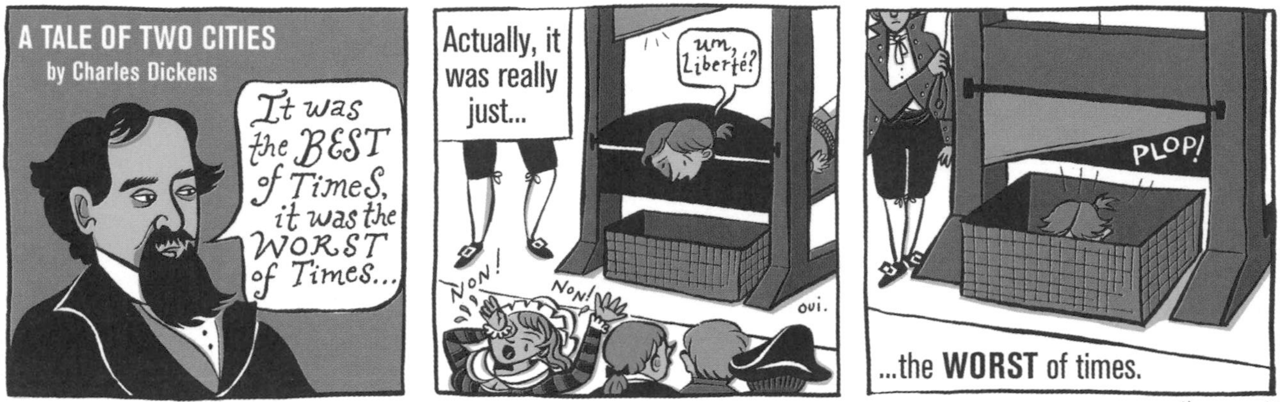
A TALE OF TWO CITIES
by Charles Dickens
It was the BEST of Times, it was the WORST of Times...
Actually, it was really just...
um, Liberté?
NON!
NON!
OUI.
PLOP!
...the WORST of times.

SEE "EPIC"

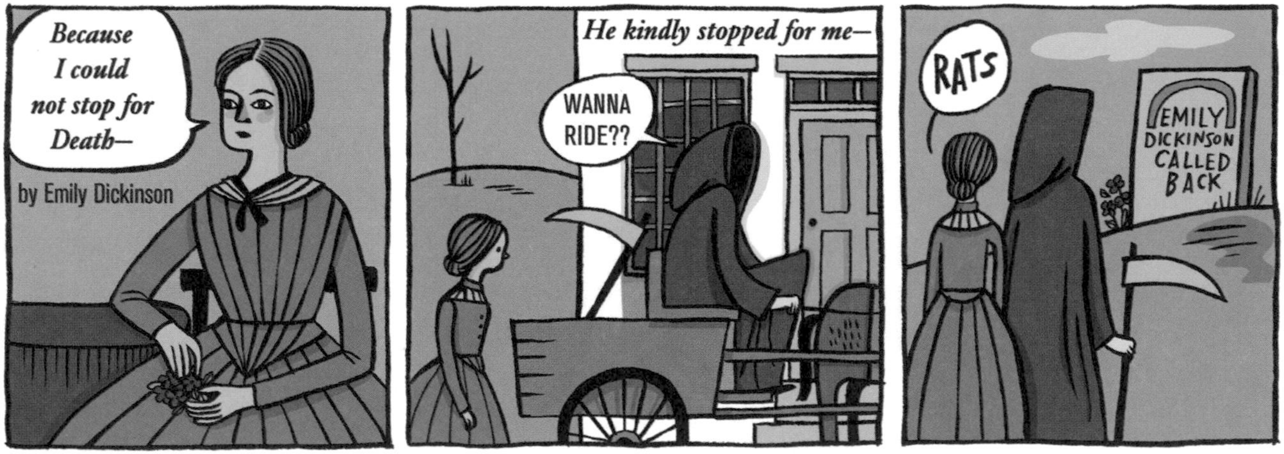
Because I could not stop for Death–
by Emily Dickinson
He kindly stopped for me–
WANNA RIDE??
RATS
EMILY DICKINSON CALLED BACK

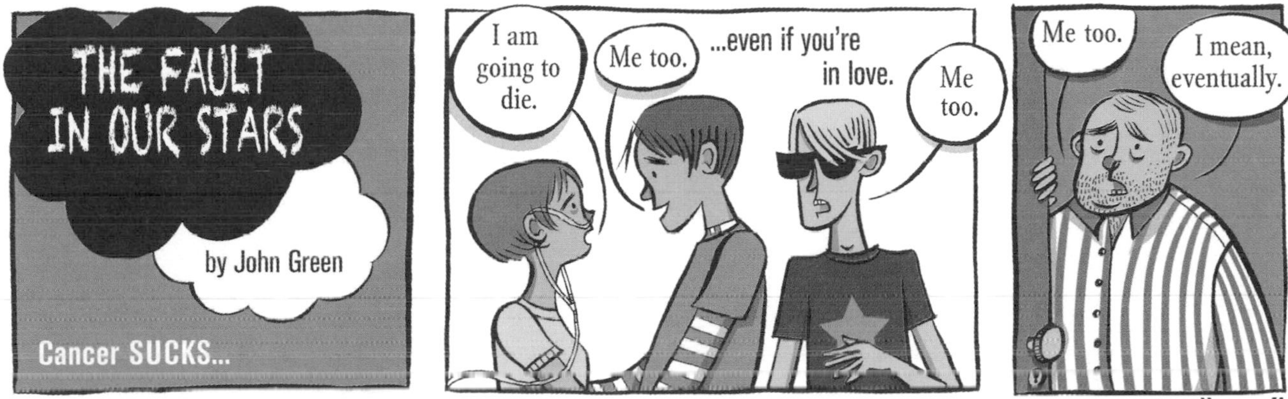
THE FAULT IN OUR STARS
by John Green
Cancer SUCKS...
I am going to die.
Me too.
...even if you're in love.
Me too.
Me too.
I mean, eventually.

SEE "SEX"

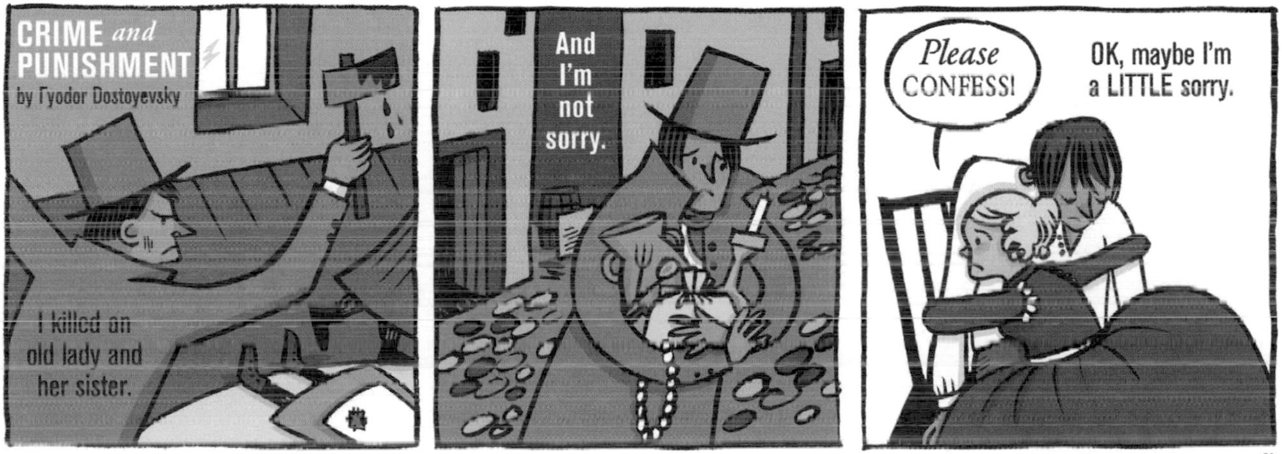
CRIME and PUNISHMENT
by Fyodor Dostoyevsky
I killed an old lady and her sister.
And I'm not sorry.
Please CONFESS!
OK, maybe I'm a LITTLE sorry.

SEE "THOUGHTS"

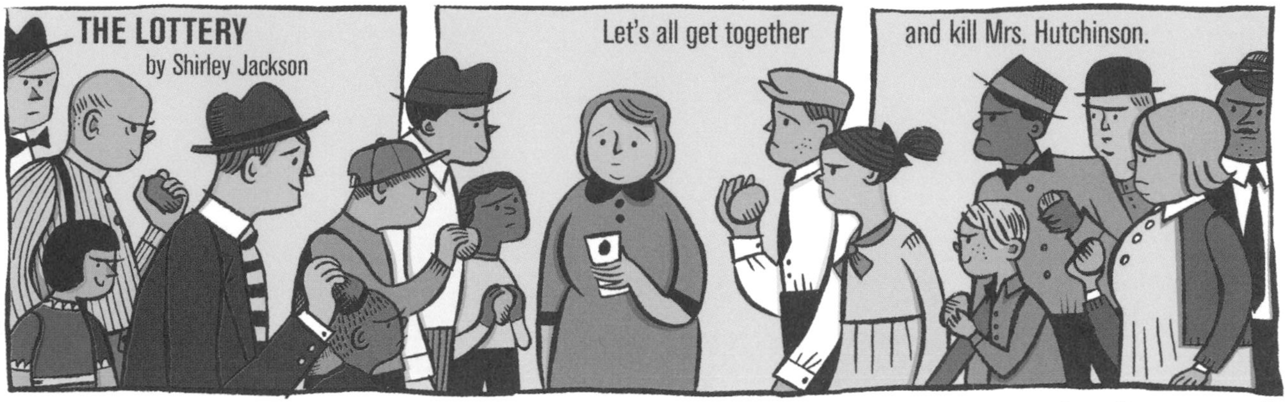
THE LOTTERY
by Shirley Jackson
Let's all get together
and kill Mrs. Hutchinson.

SEE "HORROR"

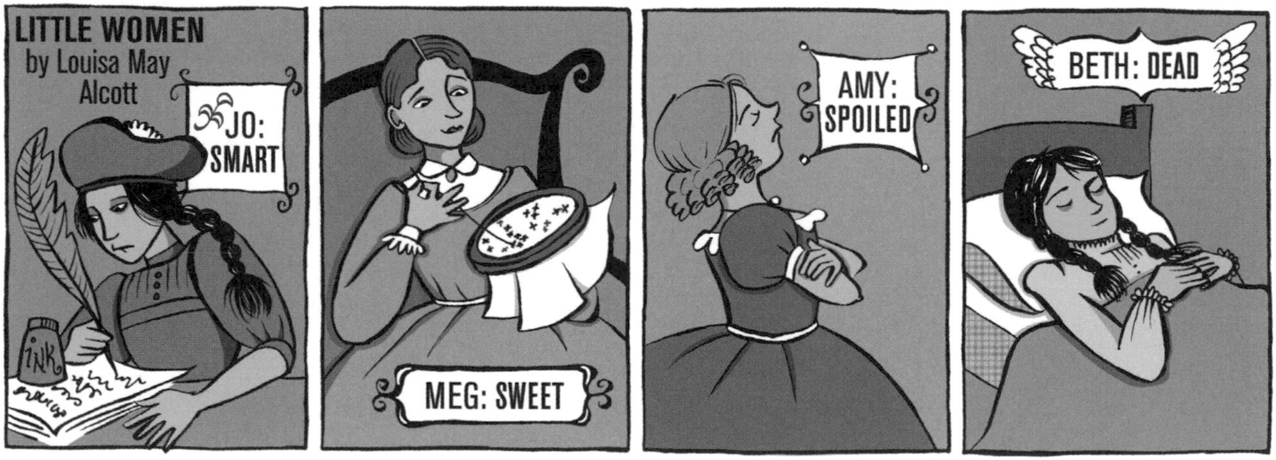
LITTLE WOMEN
by Louisa May Alcott
JO: SMART
INK
MEG: SWEET
AMY: SPOILED
BETH: DEAD

SEE "FAMILIES"

THE END

HOW TO WRITE YOUR OWN THREE-PANEL BOOK

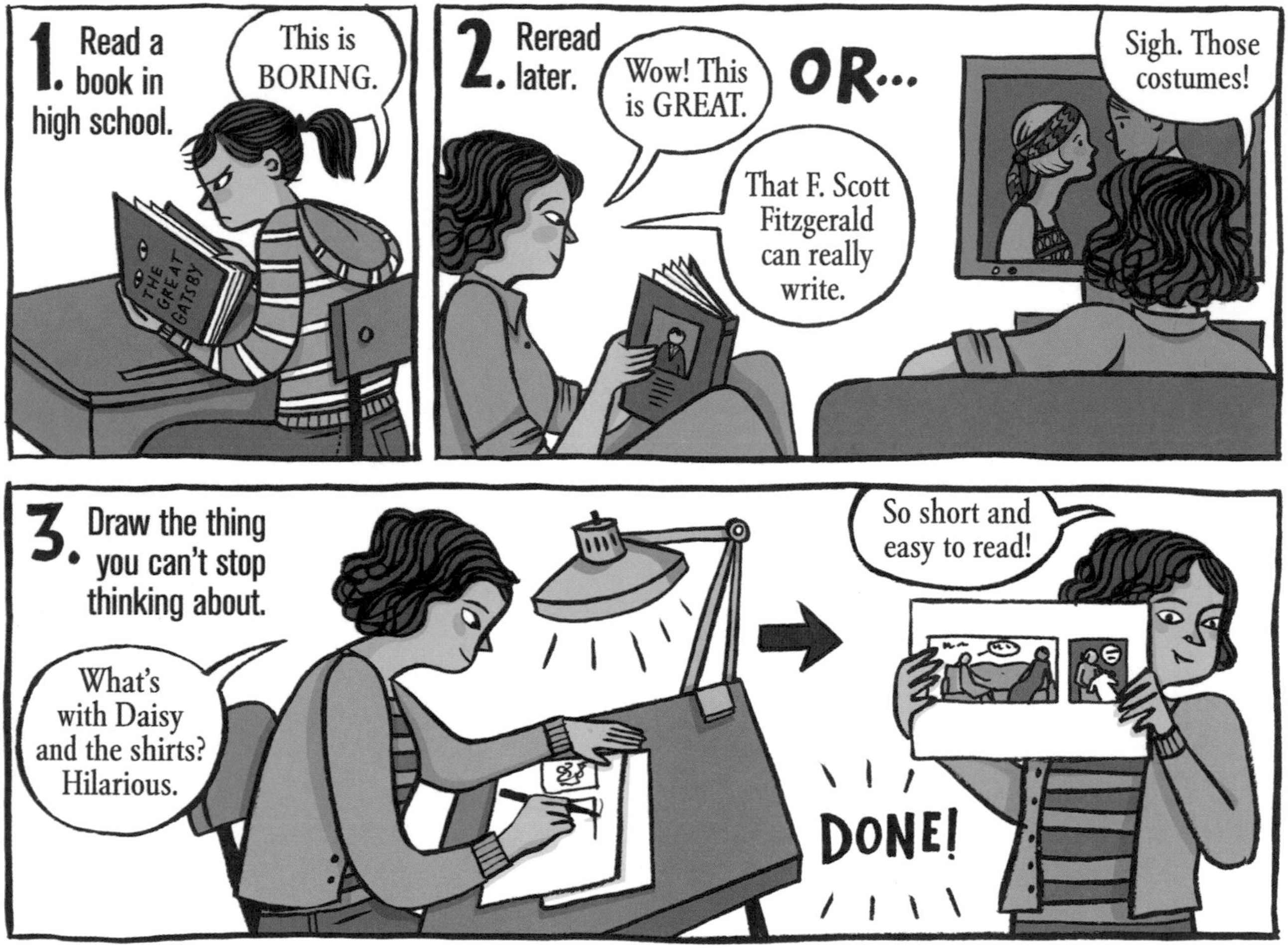
1. Read a book in high school.
This is BORING.
THE GREAT GATSBY
2. Reread later.
Wow! This is GREAT.
That F. Scott Fitzgerald can really write.
OR...
Sigh. Those costumes!
3. Draw the thing you can't stop thinking about.
What's with Daisy and the shirts? Hilarious.
So short and easy to read!
DONE!

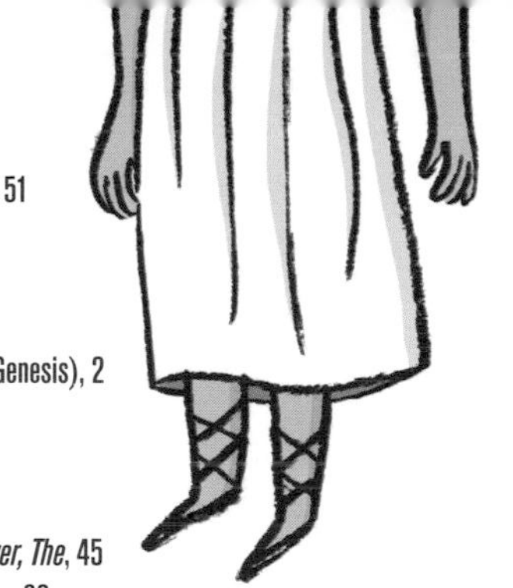

INDEX BY TITLE

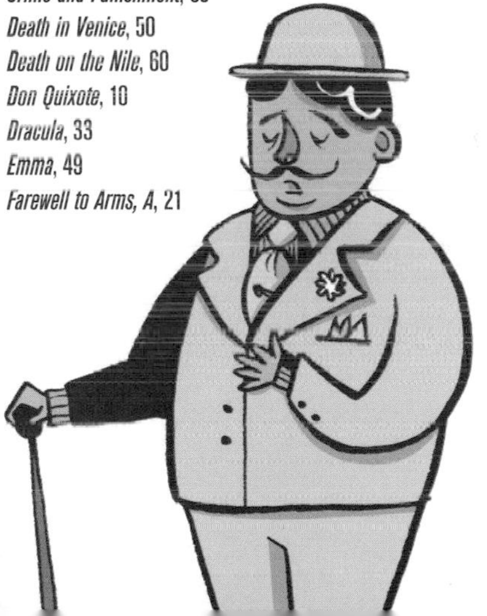

INDEX

BY SUBJECT

I am DEAD.

INDEX
BY SUBJECT

ACKNOWLEDGMENTS

Thank you to all those wonderful people who've helped
me with these comics along the way:

Kristine Brogno
David and Barbara Brown
Joanna Cotler
Amy Gash
Elise Howard
Regan McMahon
John McMurtrie
Elisabeth Scharlatt
Samatha Schoech
Charlotte Sheedy
Oscar Villalon
Laura Williams
Mo Willems
Suzi Young

and Daniel and
Otto Handler,
of course.

LISA BROWN

Is a *New York Times* bestselling illustrator, author, and cartoonist. Her slew of works for young readers includes the picture books *The Airport Book*; *How to Be*; *Goldfish Ghost*, by Lemony Snicket; *Mummy Cat*, by Marcus Ewert; and her first graphic novel, *The Phantom Twin*. She is married to the novelist Daniel Handler and lives with him and their teenage son in San Francisco, where she teaches in the illustration department of the California College of the Arts. You can find Lisa Brown online at americanchickens.com.

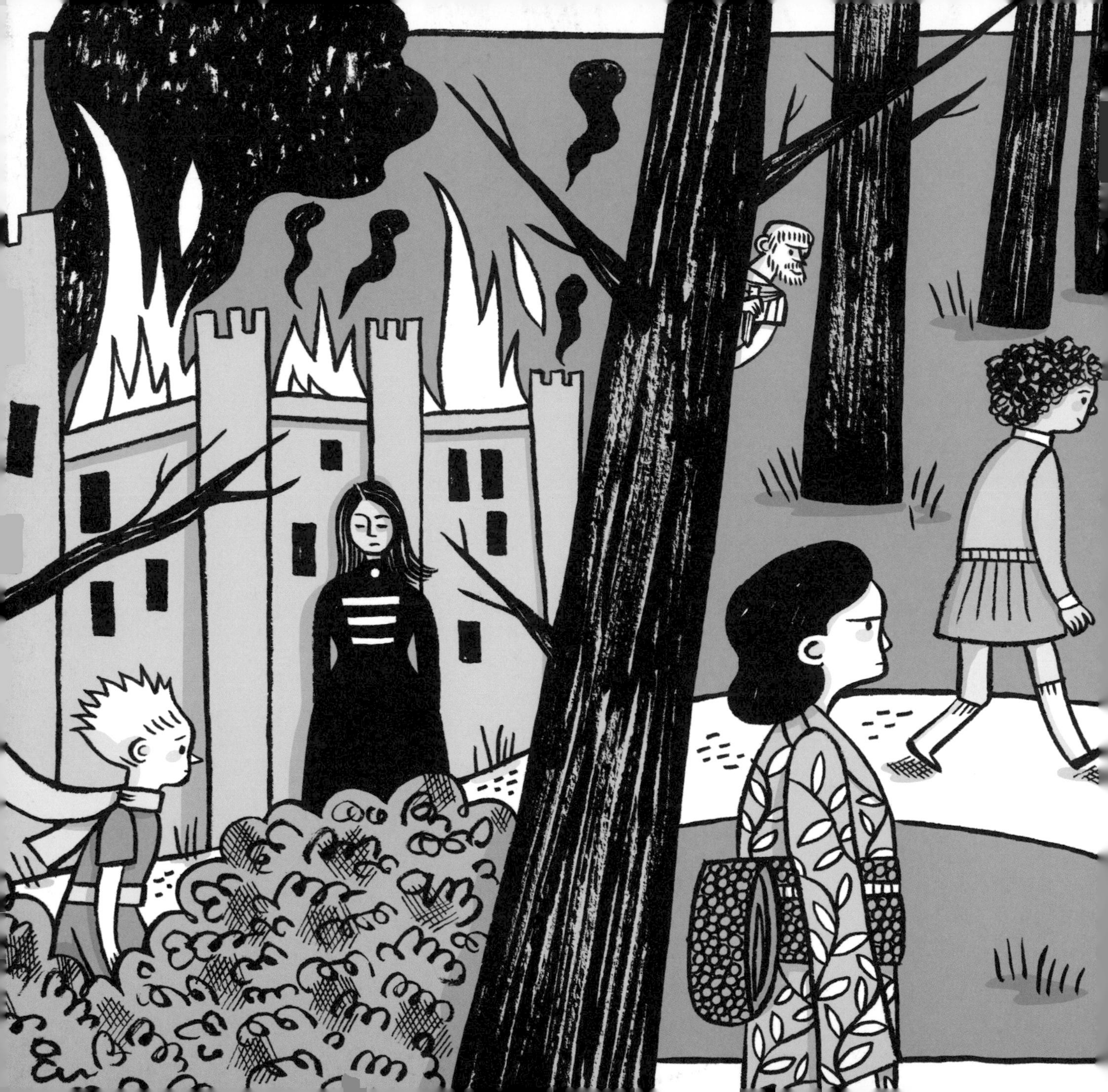

31472400070789

I0819627

Good Night, Baby Bear

FRANK ASCH

Voyager Books

Harcourt, Inc.

Orlando   Austin   New York   San Diego   London

Requests for permission to make copies of any part of the work should be submitted online at
www.harcourt.com/contact or mailed to: Permissions Department, Harcourt, Inc.,
6277 Sea Harbor Drive, Orlando, Florida 32887-6777.

www.HarcourtBooks.com

First Voyager Books edition 2001
Voyager Books is a trademark of Harcourt, Inc., registered in the United States of America
and/or other jurisdictions.

The Library of Congress has cataloged the hardcover edition as follows:
Asch, Frank.
Good night, Baby Bear/written and illustrated by Frank Asch.
p. cm.
Summary: As winter approaches, Mother Bear must bring a snack, a drink,
and finally the moon to her cub before he can go to sleep in a cave.
[1. Bears—Fiction. 2. Sleep—Fiction. 3. Bedtime—Fiction. 4. Mother and child—Fiction.] I. Title.
PZ7.A778Gof 1998
[E]—dc21   96-39178
ISBN 978-0-15-200836-9
ISBN 978-0-15-216368-6 pb

TWP   12 11 10 9 8 7
4500228303

The paintings in this book were made with brushes
and sponges using Cel-Vinyl acrylic paint on bristol board.
The display type was set in Esprit.
The text type was set in Goudy Catalogue.
Color separations by Tien Wah Press, Singapore
Printed and bound by Tien Wah Press, Singapore
Production supervision by Sandy Grebenar and Wendi Taylor
Designed by Lydia D'moch

To my mother, Margaret Asch
1916–1997

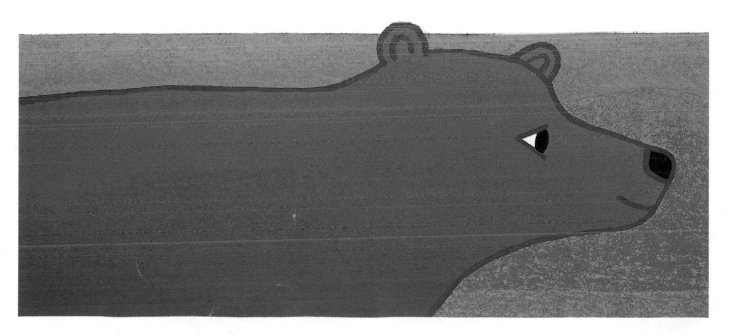

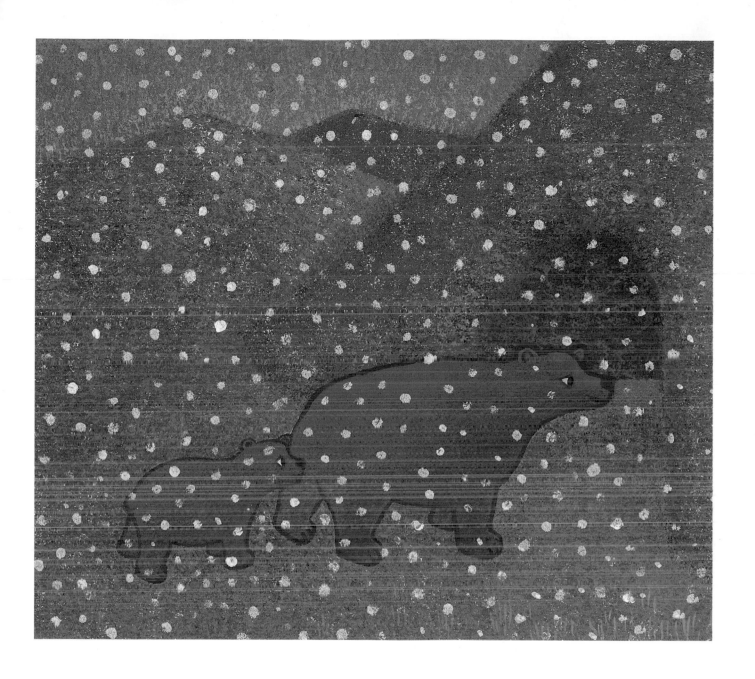

One chilly night as snow began to fall, Mother Bear led
Baby Bear to a cave.

"This is where we'll sleep through the winter," said
Mother Bear.

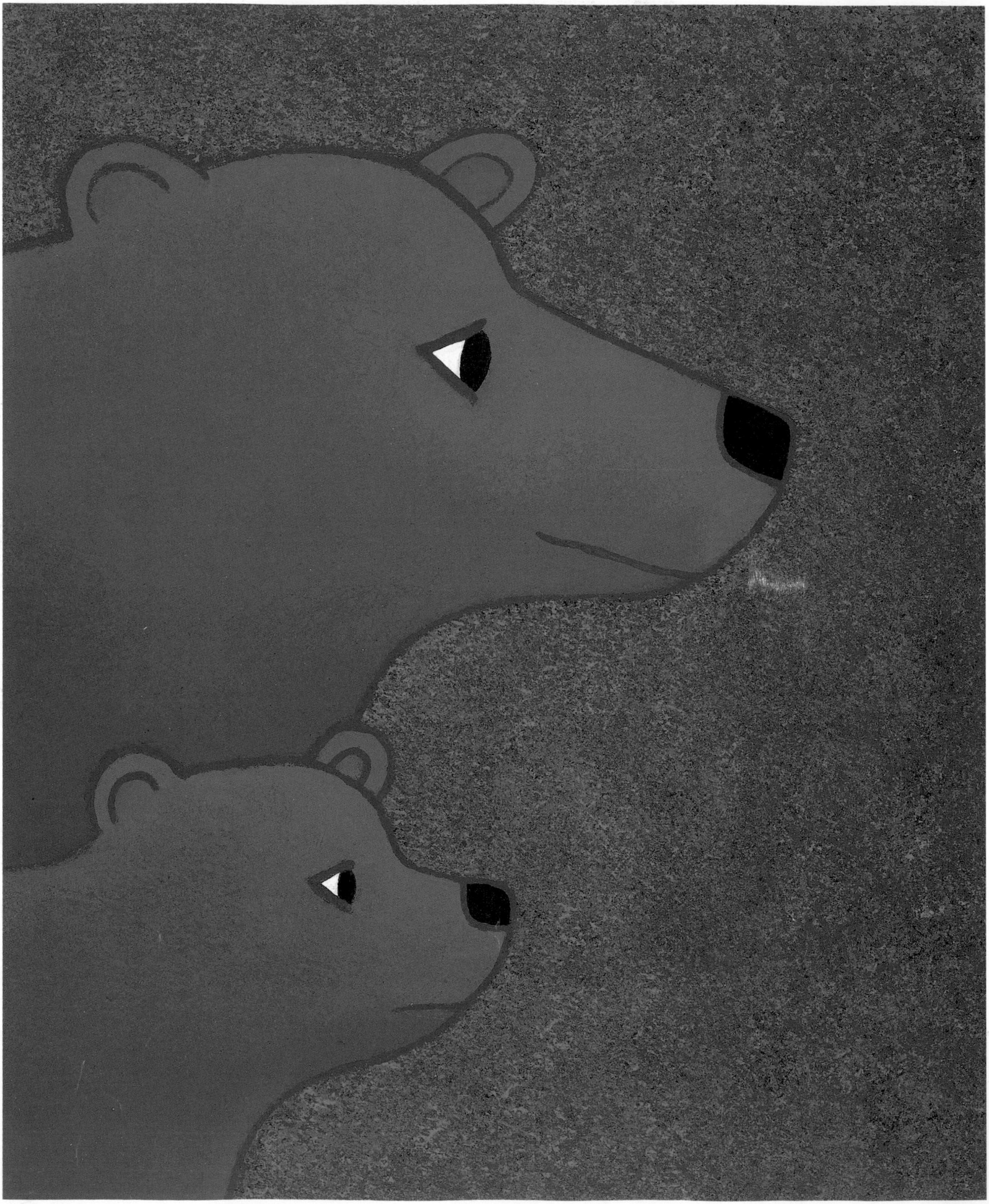

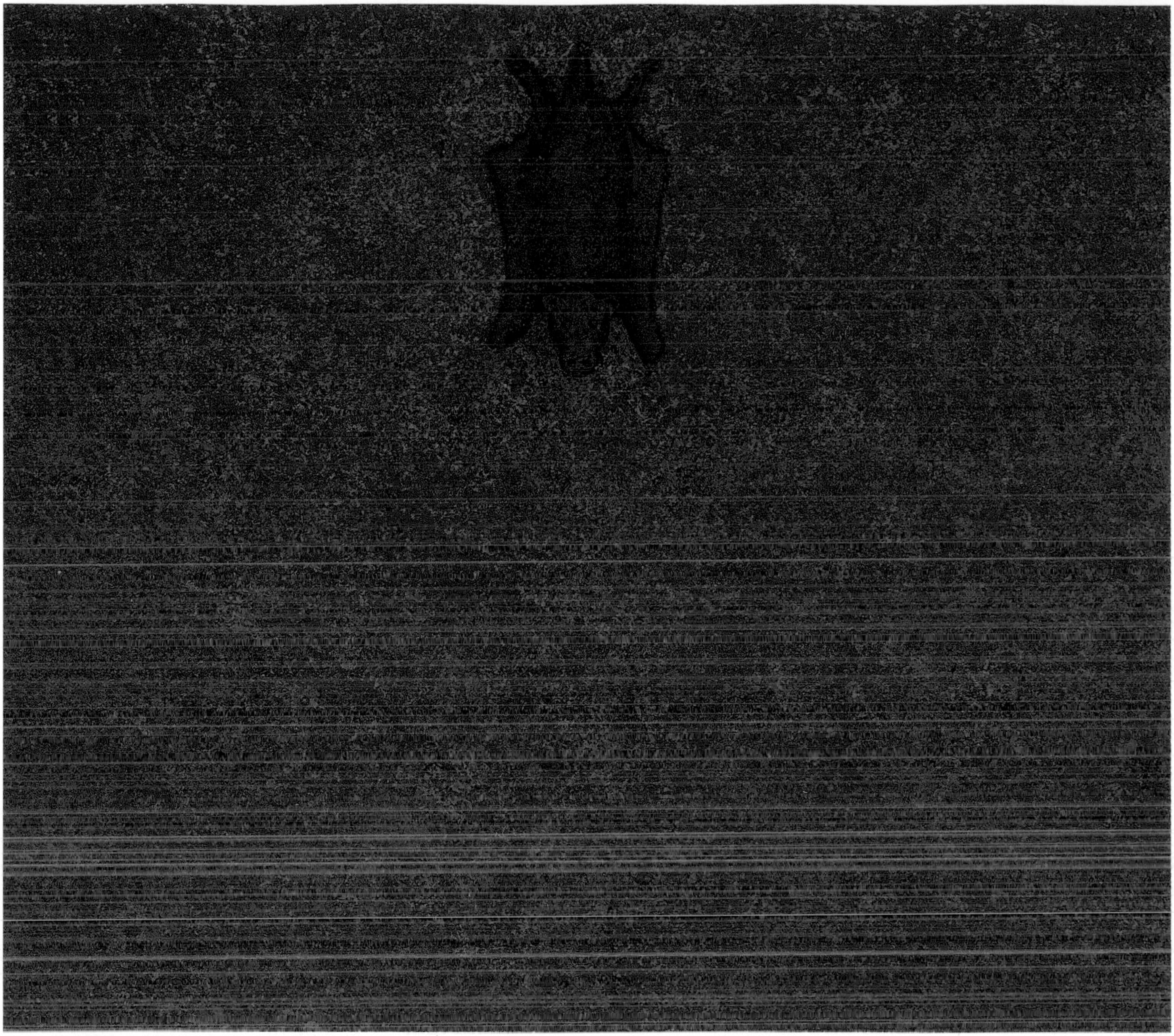

Baby Bear wasn't used to sleeping in a cave. "Why can't we sleep under the sky like we always do?" he asked.

"Winter has just begun," replied Mother Bear. "Soon it will be too cold to sleep under the sky."

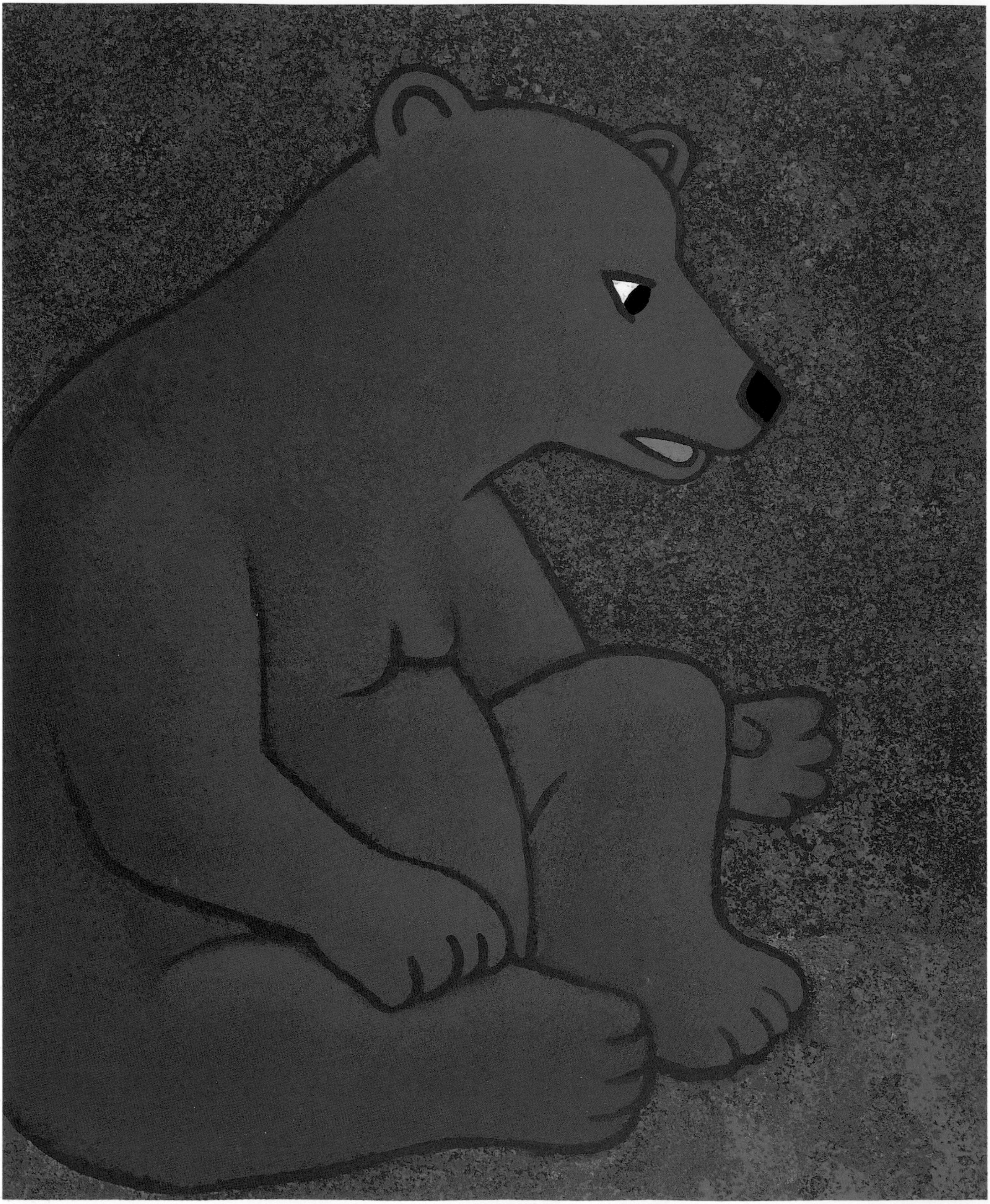

“Mama, I’m hungry,” said Baby Bear.

“I’m sorry, there’s no food in the cave,” replied Mother Bear.

“But I always had a little snack before bedtime when we slept outside,” said Baby Bear.

“Mmmm.” Mother Bear thought for a moment. “Wait here. I’ll be right back.”

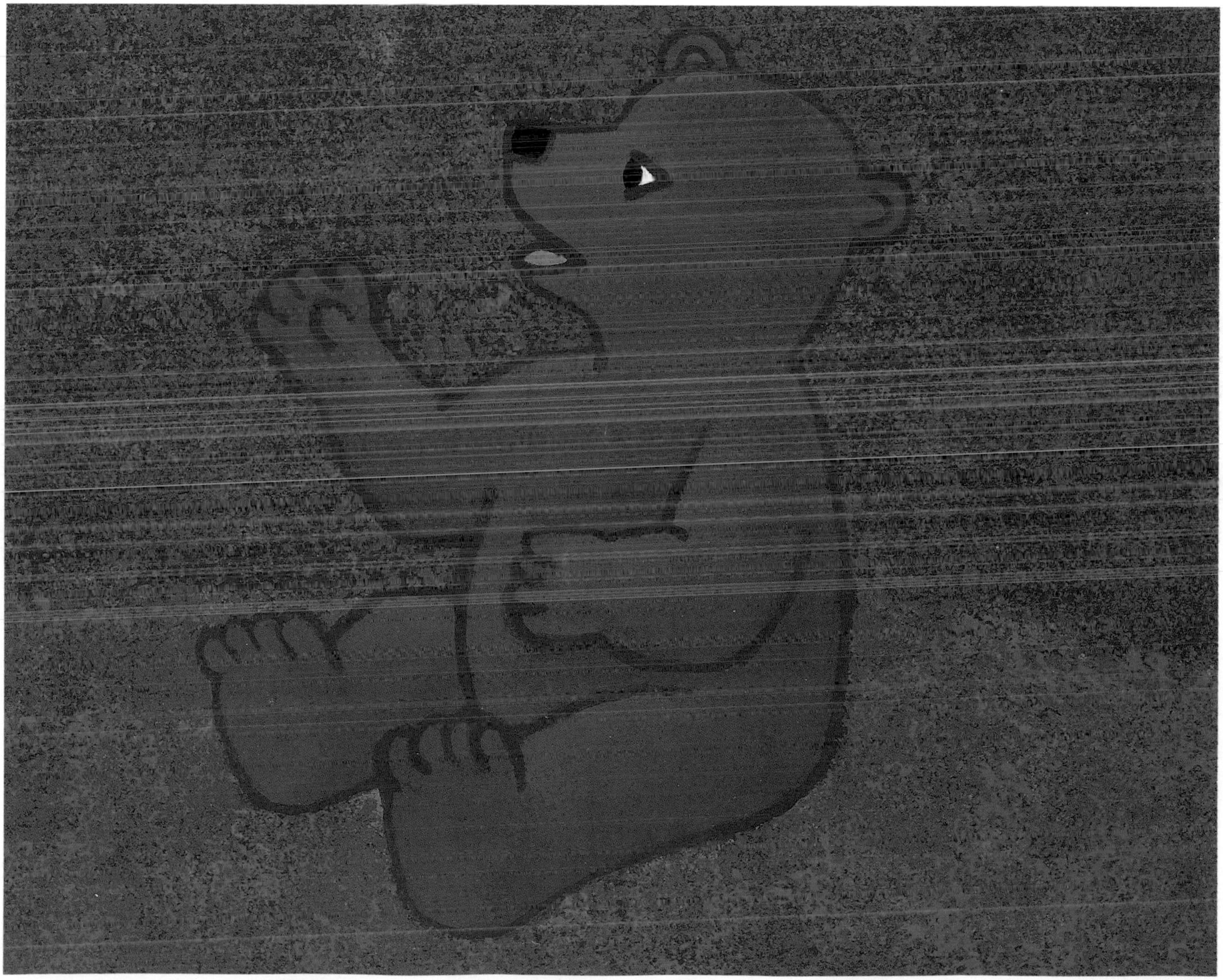

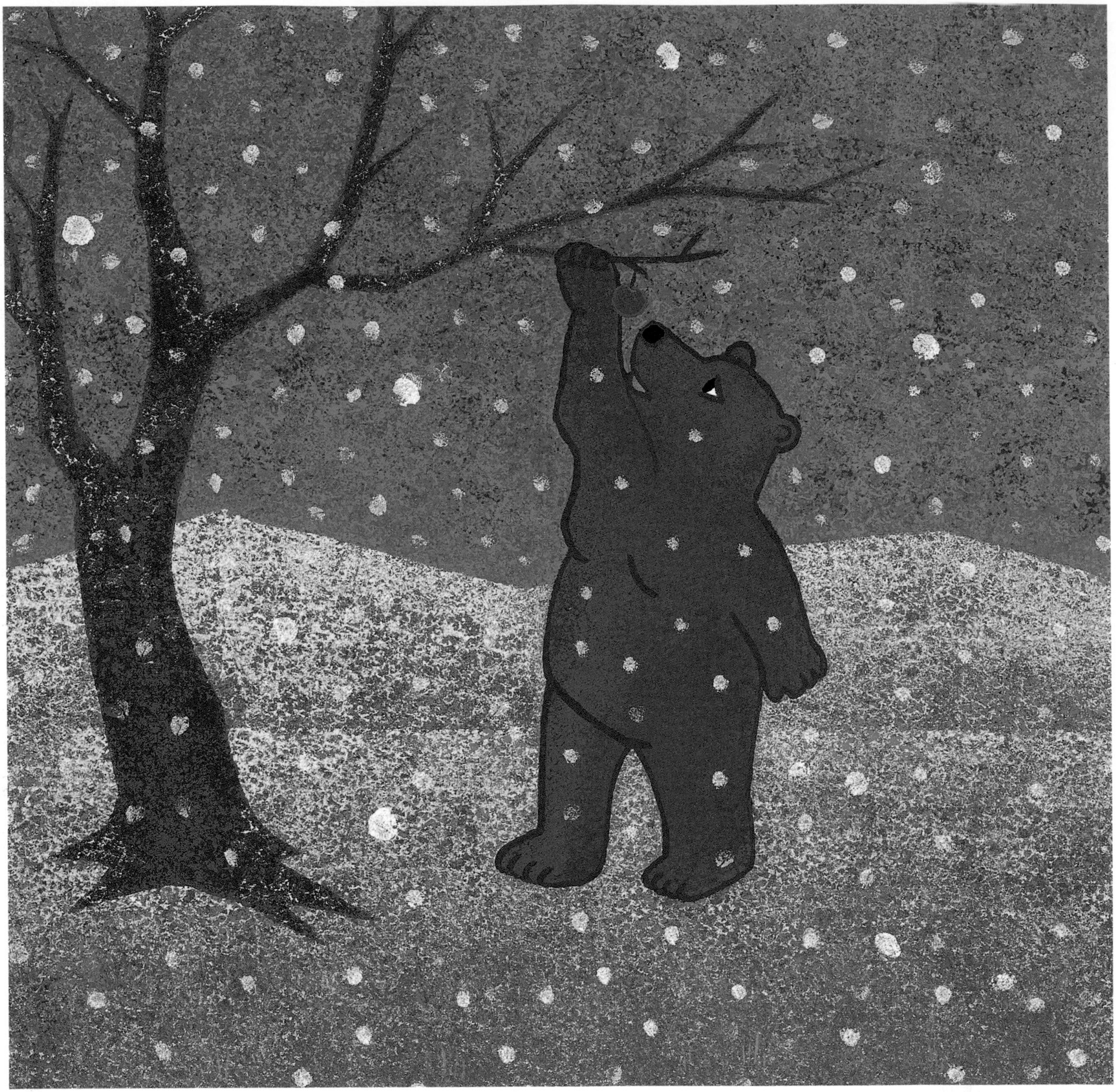

Not far from the cave, Mother Bear found an old apple tree.

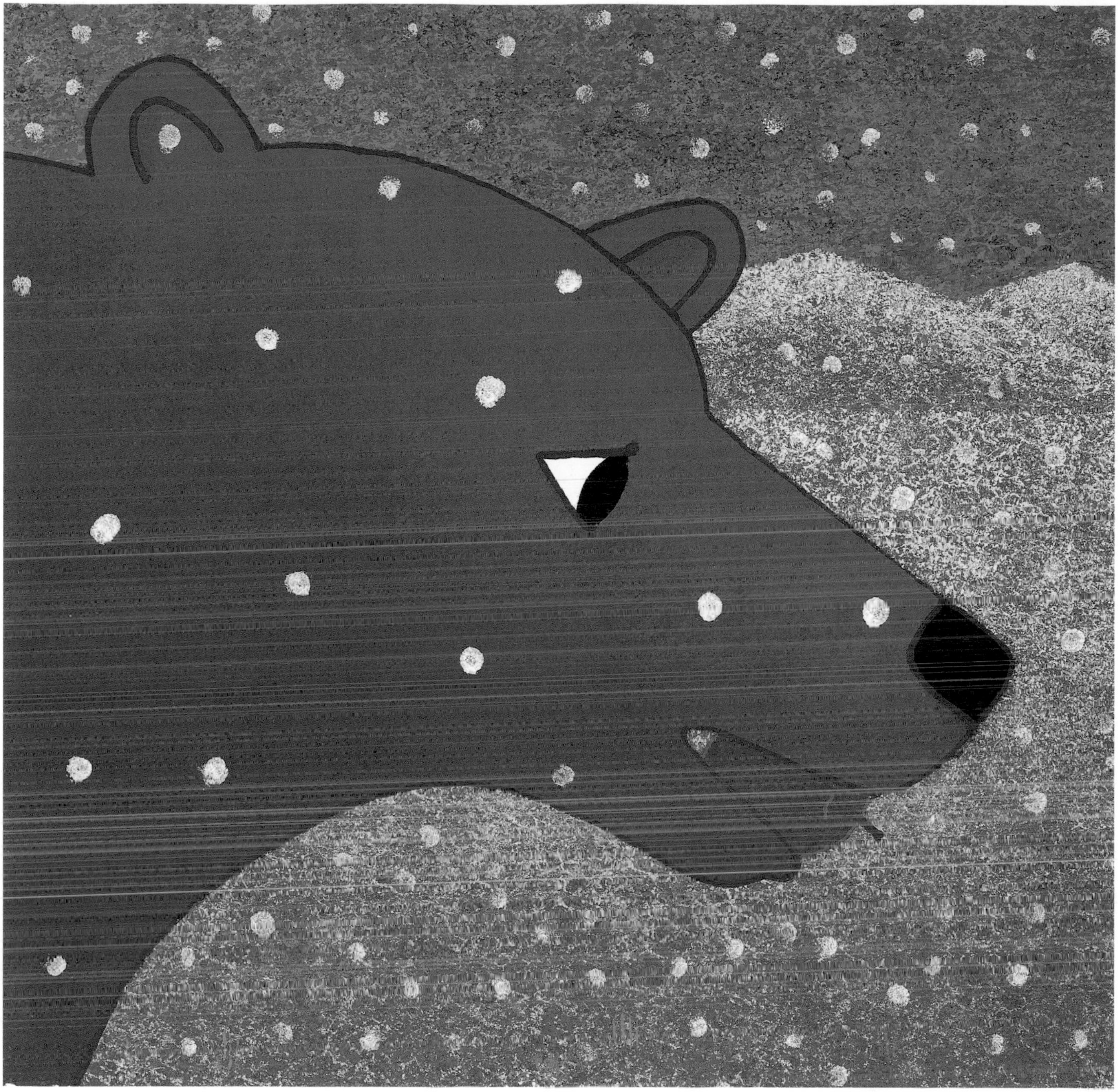

She pulled down a branch, plucked an apple, and carried it back to her cub.

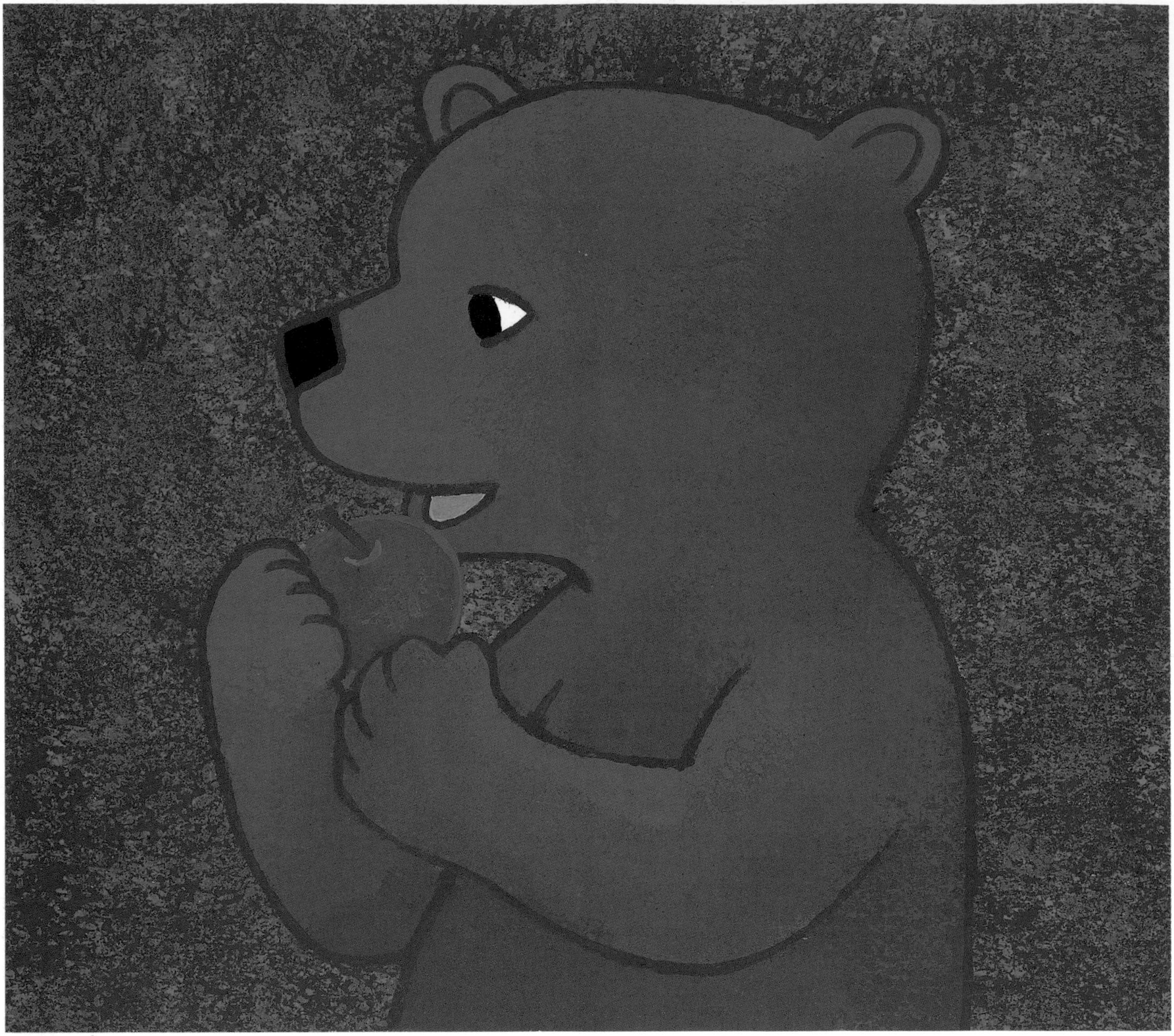

"Thank you, Mama," said Baby Bear as he munched on the apple.

Mother Bear soon fell asleep. But Baby Bear couldn't get comfortable. He *couldn't* fall asleep.

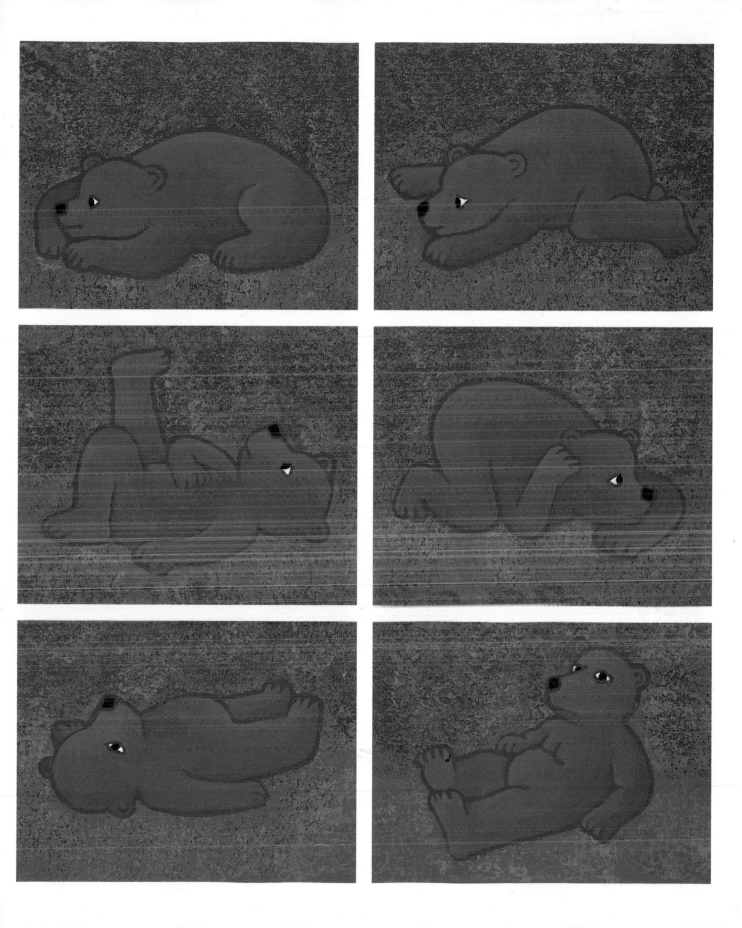

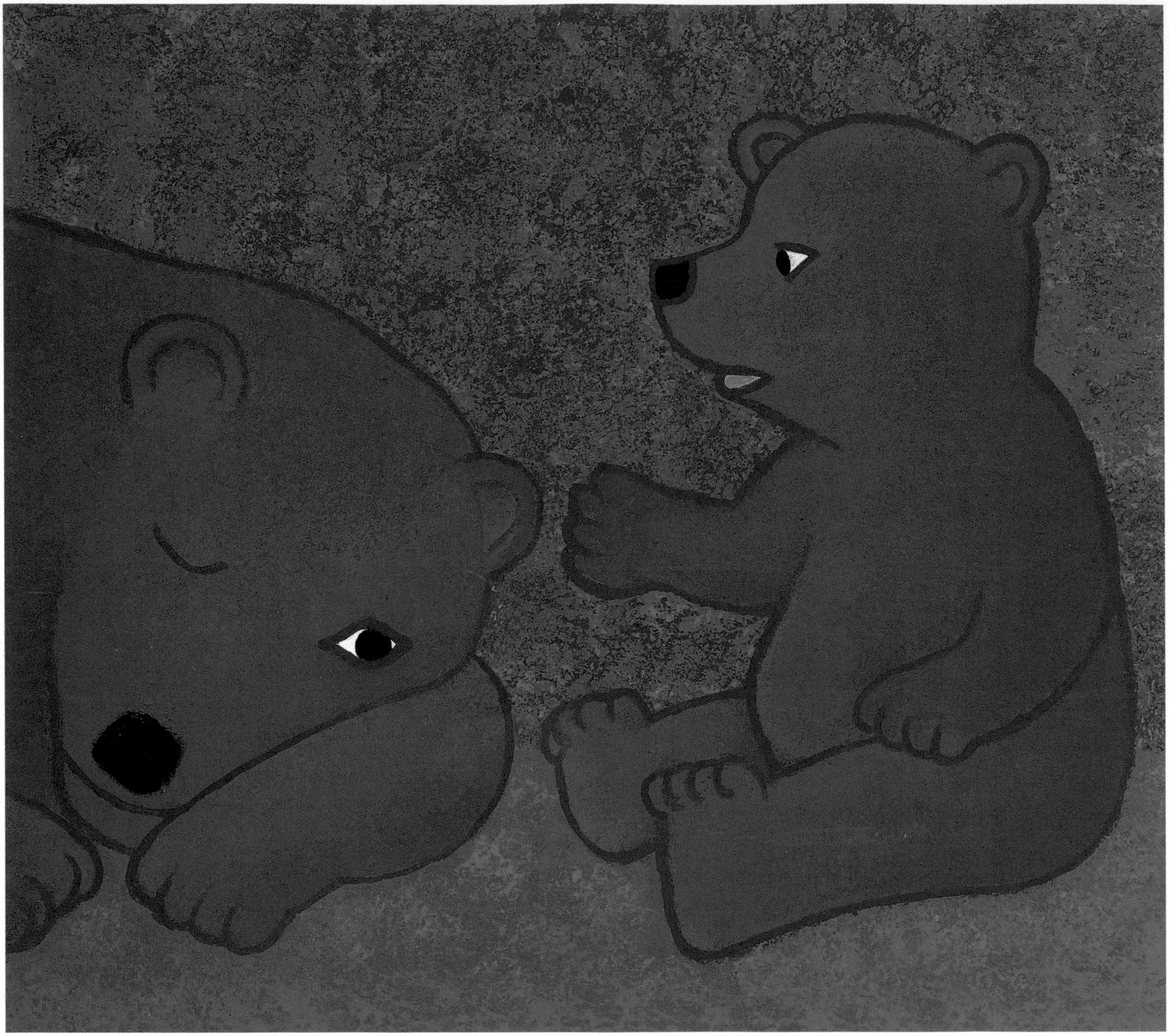

He poked Mother Bear and said, “Mama, I’m thirsty.”
“I’m sorry,” replied Mother Bear. “There’s no water in the cave.”

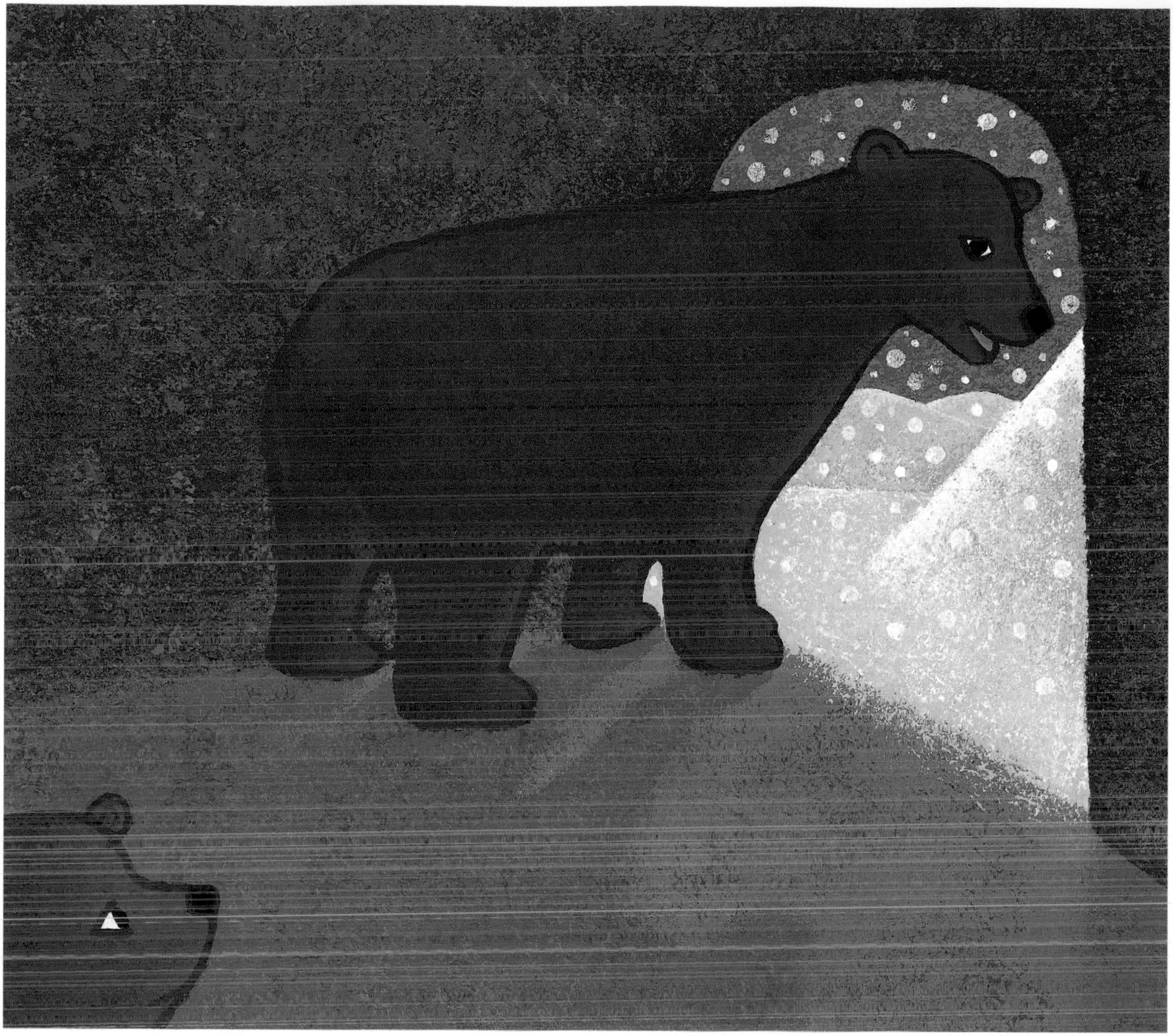

“But I always had a drink before I went to sleep when we slept under the stars,” said Baby Bear.

“Okay,” sighed Mother Bear. “Stay here, and I’ll see what I can do.”

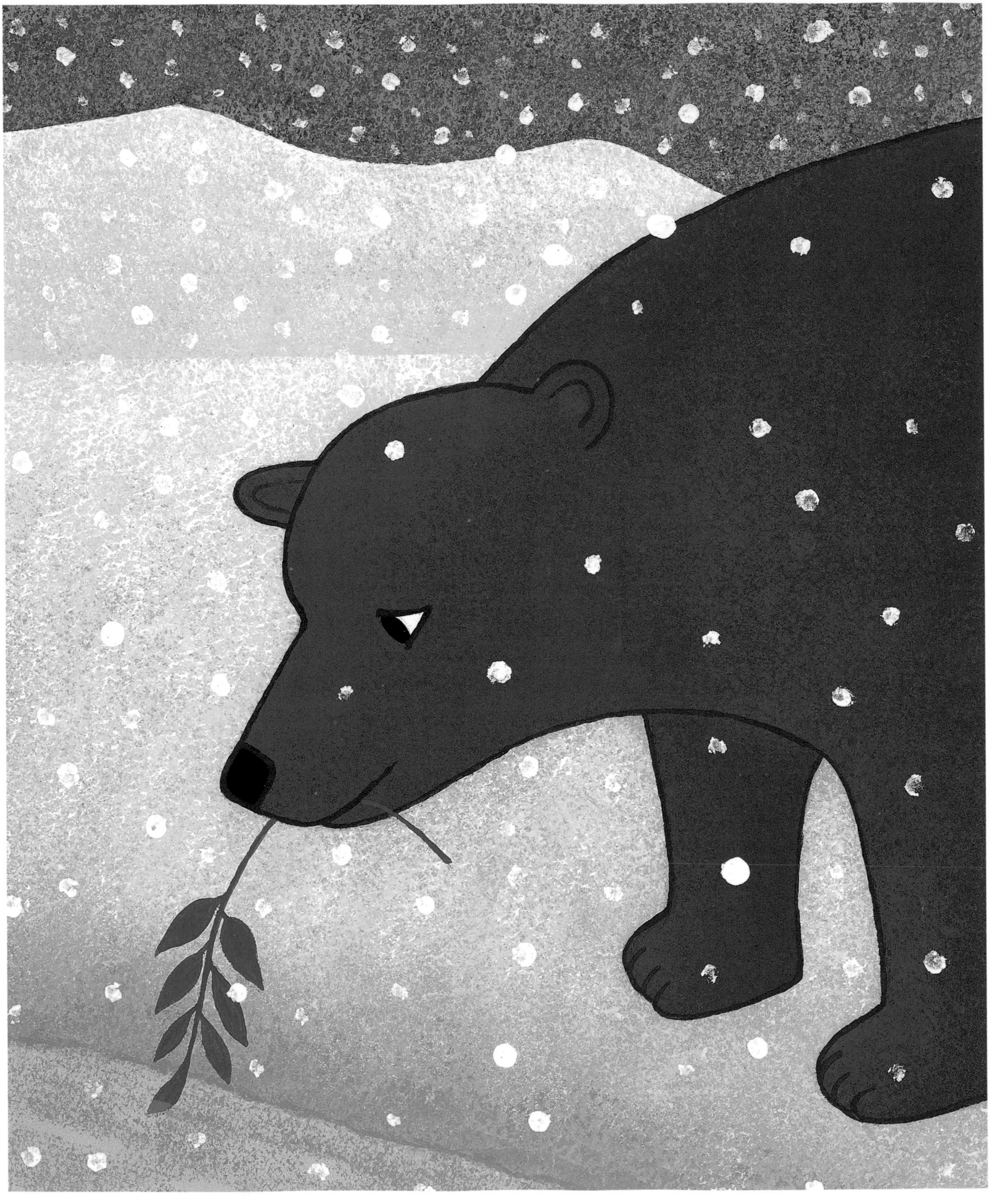

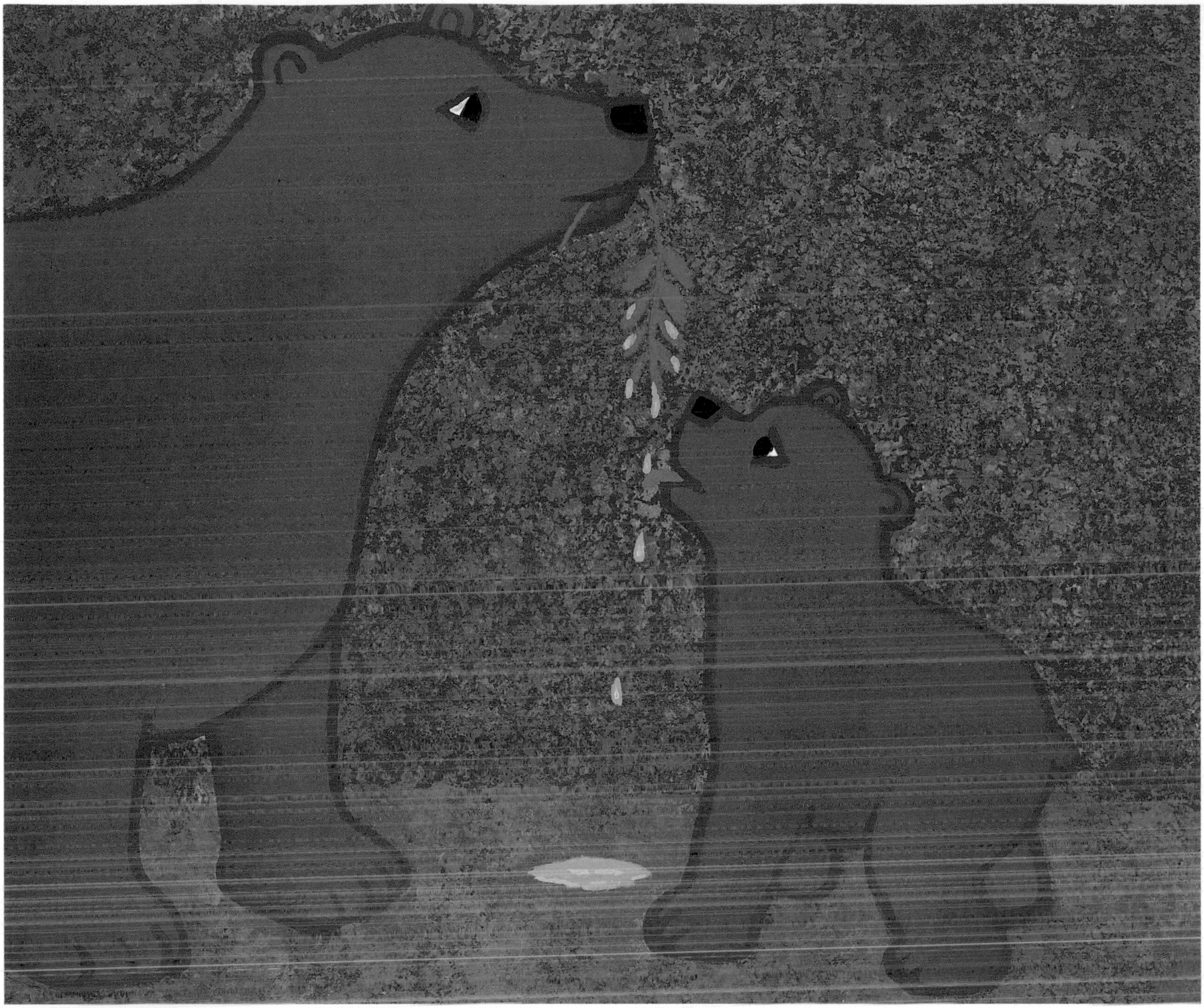

Mother Bear followed the scent of water until it led her to a small stream. She dipped some leaves into the water and carried them back to Baby Bear.

"Thank you, Mama," said Baby Bear as he licked the water from the leaves. "Maybe *now* I'll sleep."

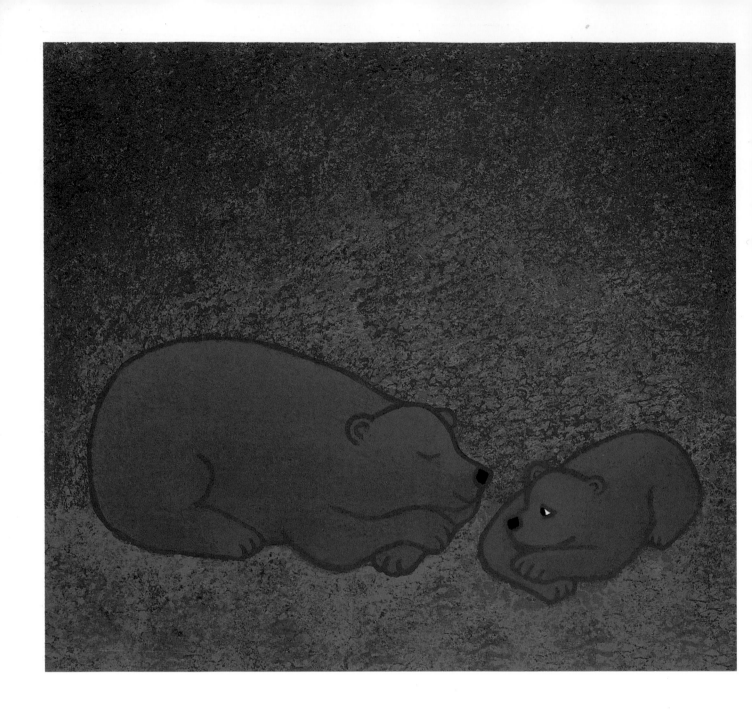

Baby Bear lay down next to Mother Bear and waited
to fall asleep.
He waited and waited and thought and thought.

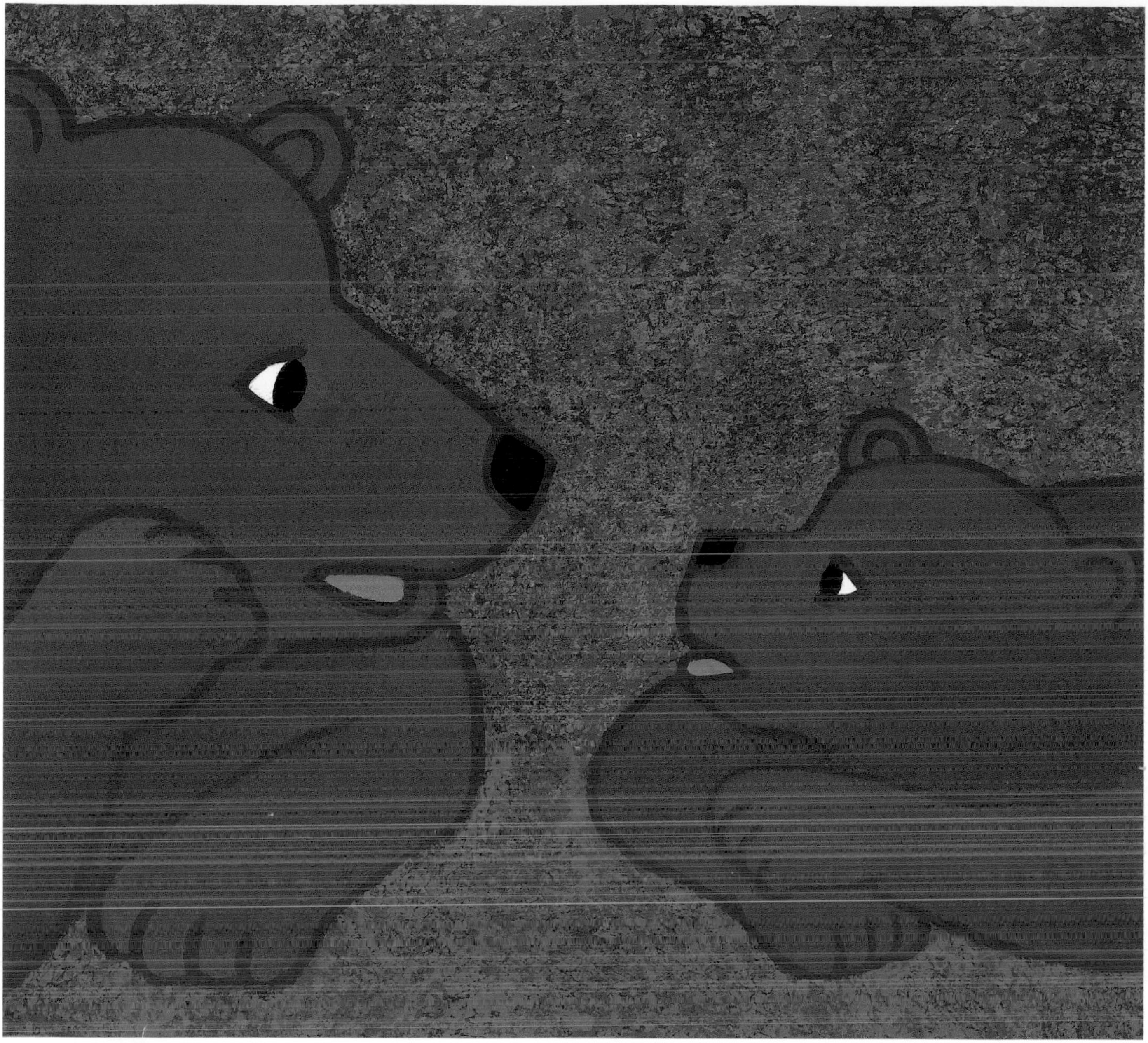

Then he bumped Mother Bear and said, "Mama, you know what I need? I need the moon."

"You need *what*?" gasped Mother Bear.

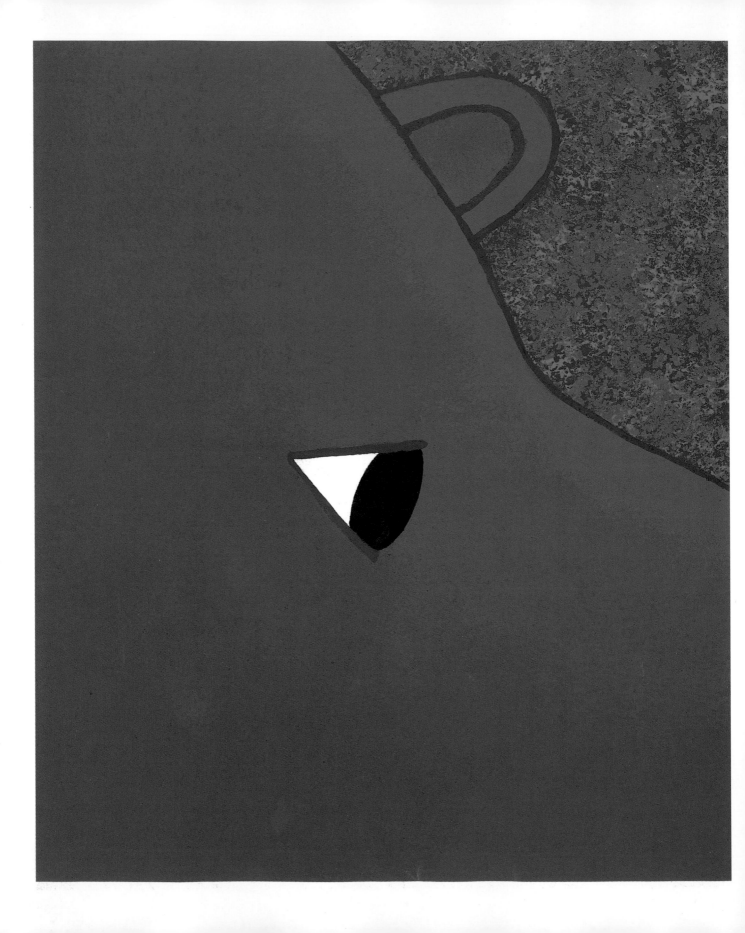

"I never have trouble falling asleep when I can look at the moon," explained Baby Bear.

"I can't get you the moon," cried Mother Bear.

"But I *need* it!" insisted Baby Bear.

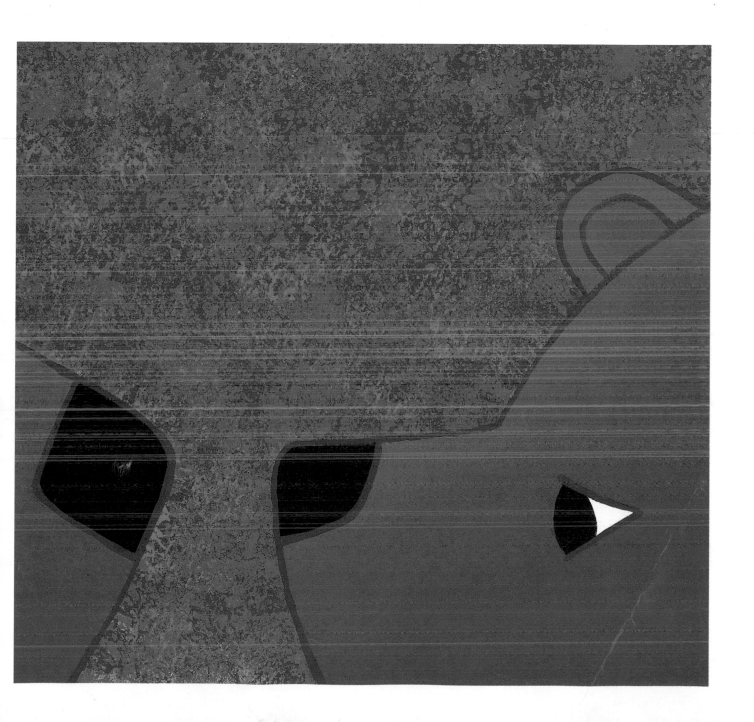

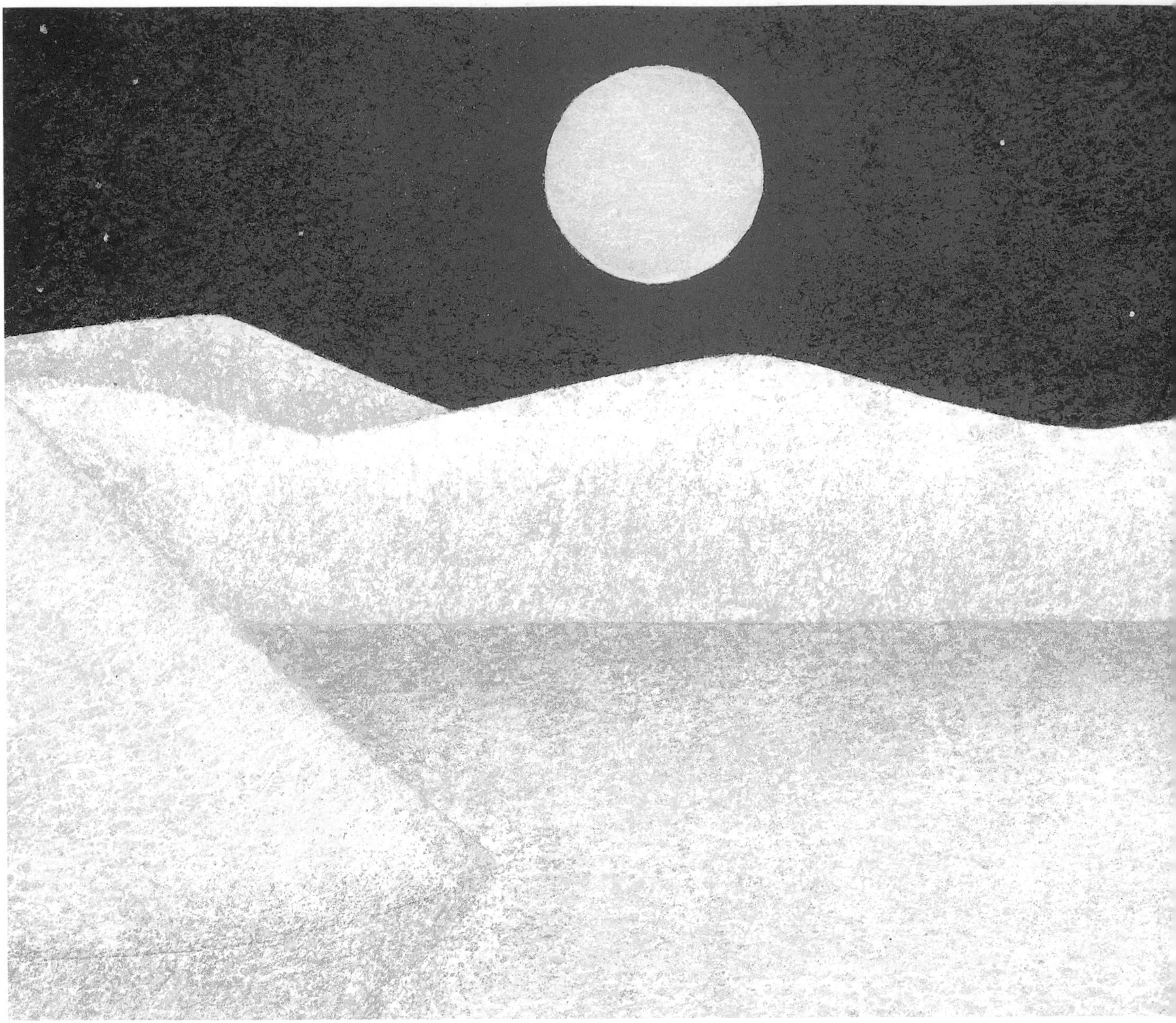

Mother Bear heaved a great sigh. “Wait here,” she said, and lumbered out of the cave.

By now the snow had stopped falling and the moon was out. Its light fell on the snow like warm honey.

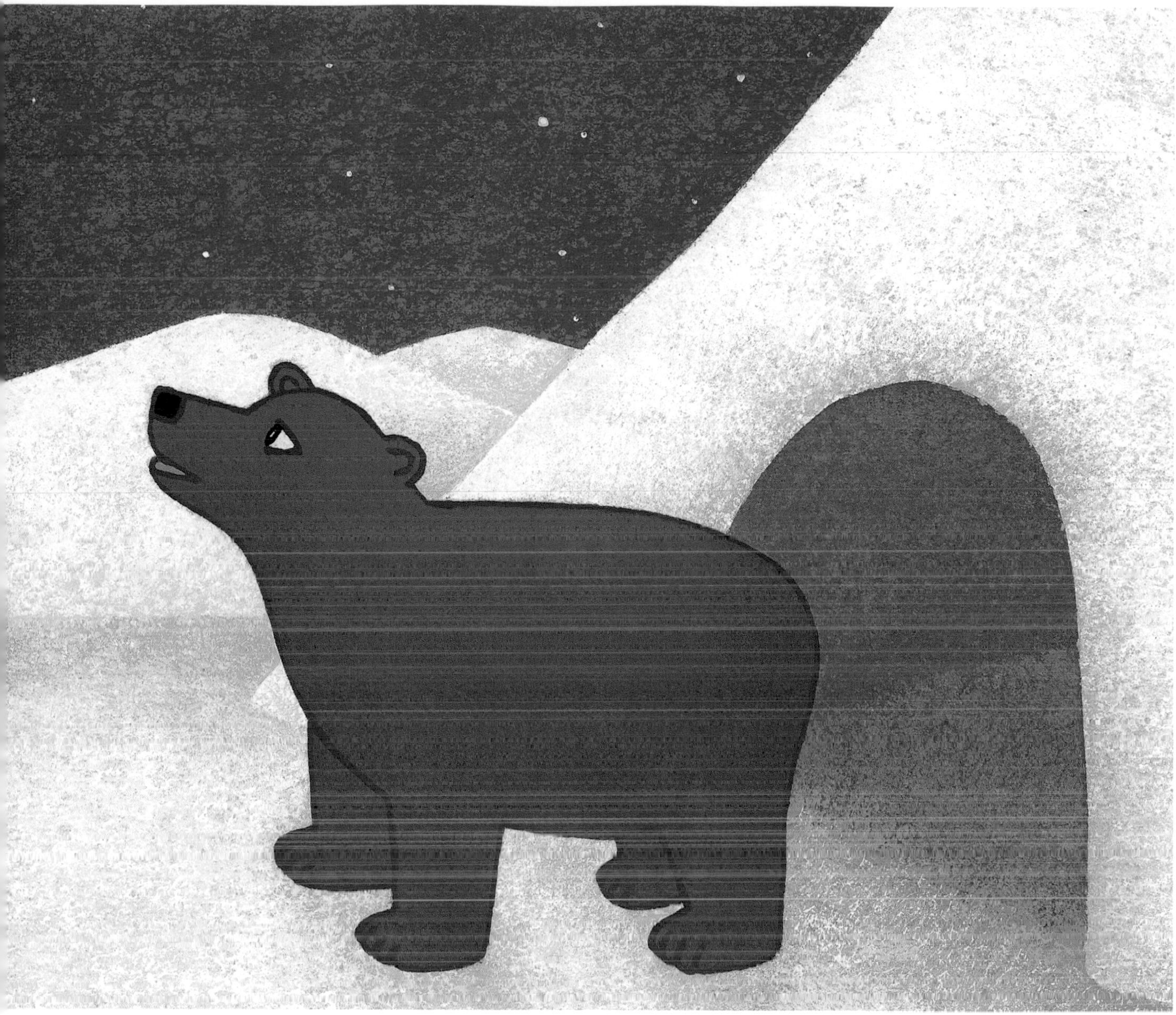

"Oh, Moon!" Mother Bear called to the sky. "I'm so tired and my baby can't fall asleep without you. What am I to do?"

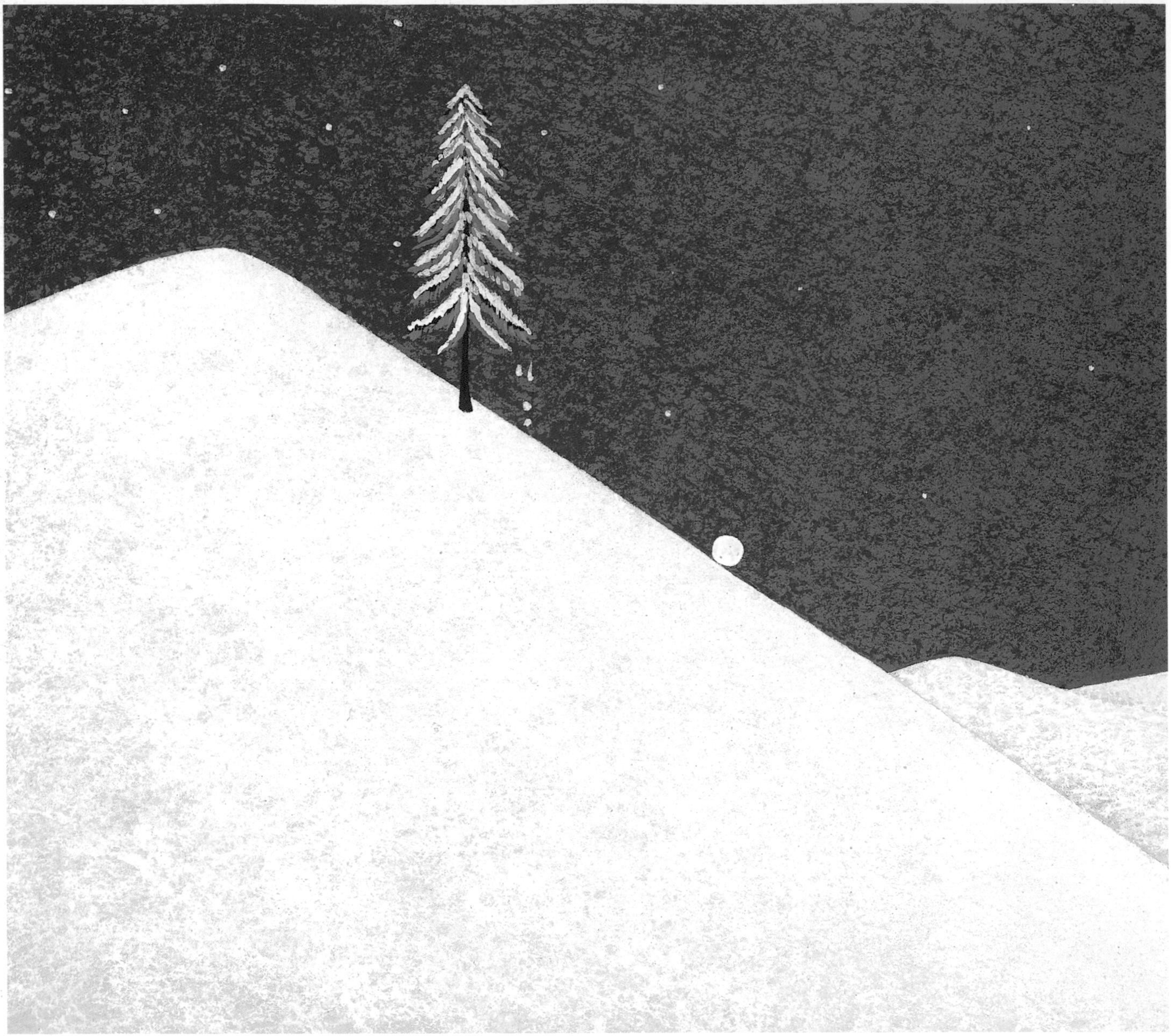

Just then some snow from a pine tree fell onto the hillside and began to roll. As it rolled it gathered more snow and grew bigger and bigger. By the time it reached Mother Bear, it looked as big and round as the moon.

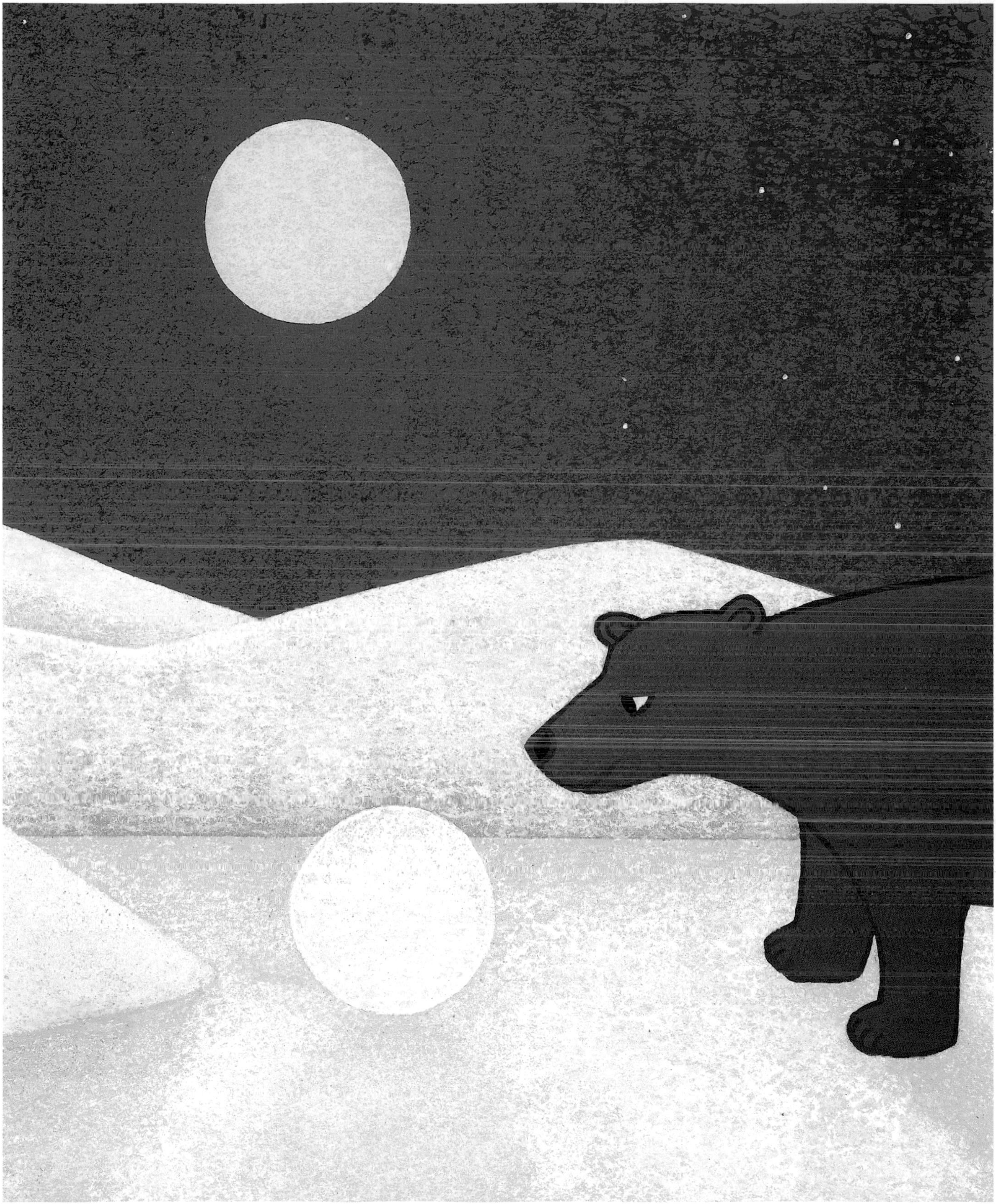

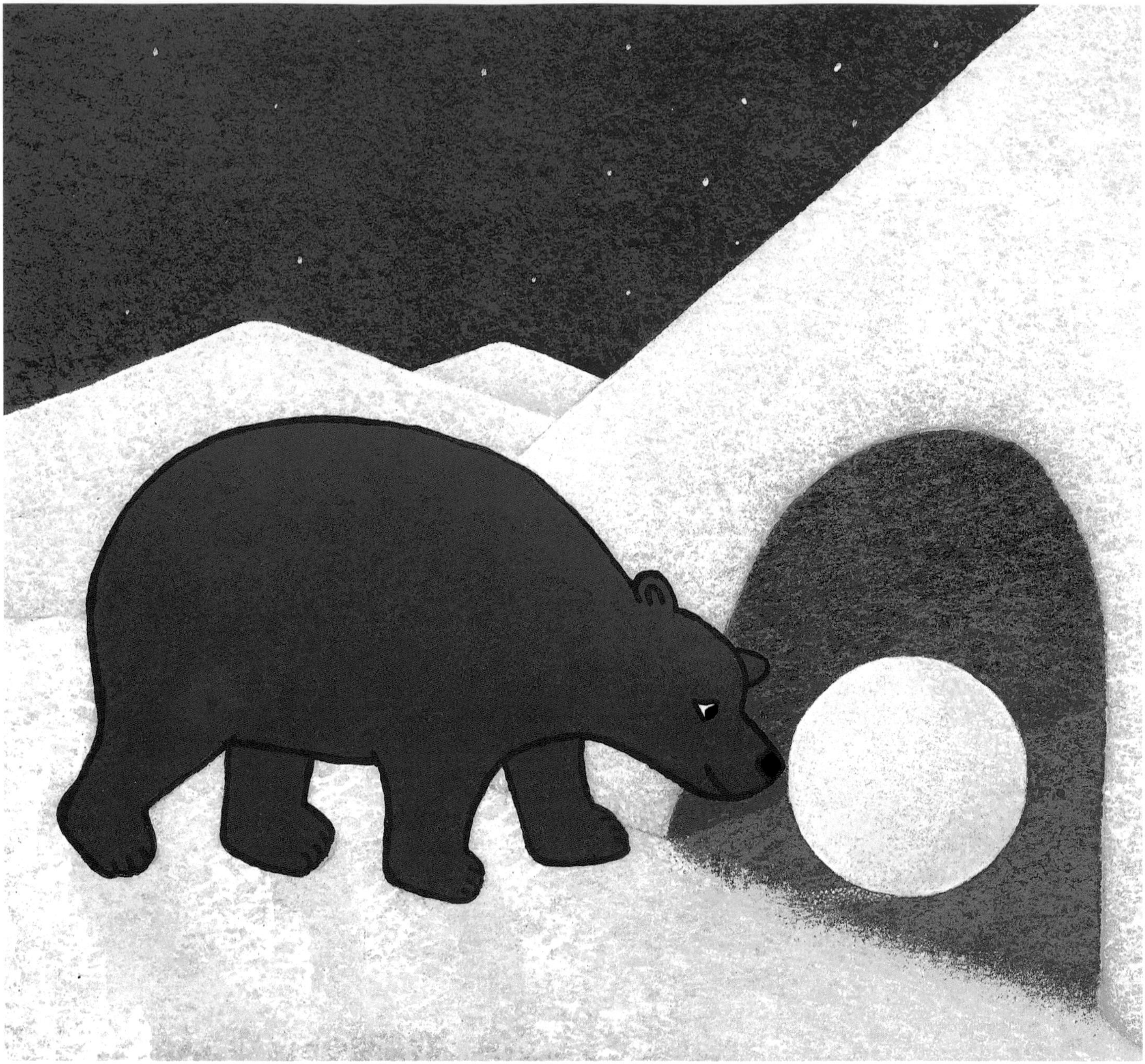

“Thank you, Moon,” said Mother Bear. And she rolled the snowball into the cave.

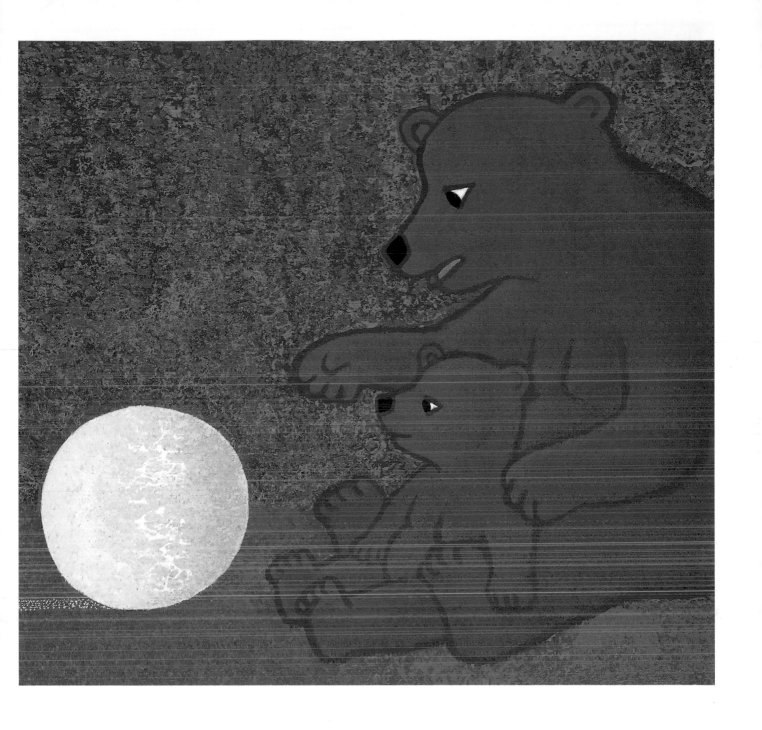

"I know it's not the moon," she said. "But there's just enough moonlight coming into the cave to make it shine like the moon. Can you see it?"

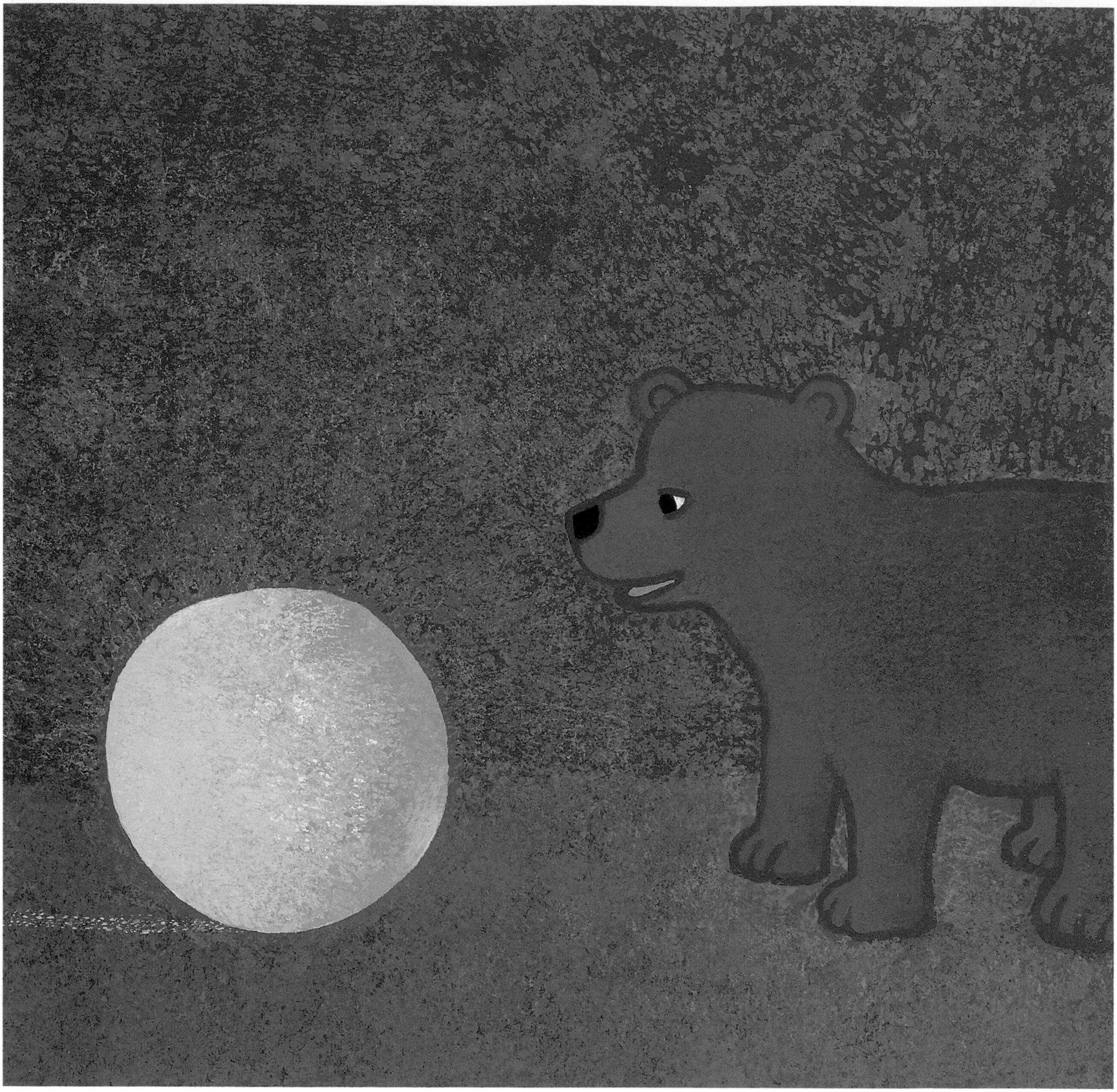

"Oh yes!" cried Baby Bear.
"Good," said Mother Bear. "Now *please* go to sleep."

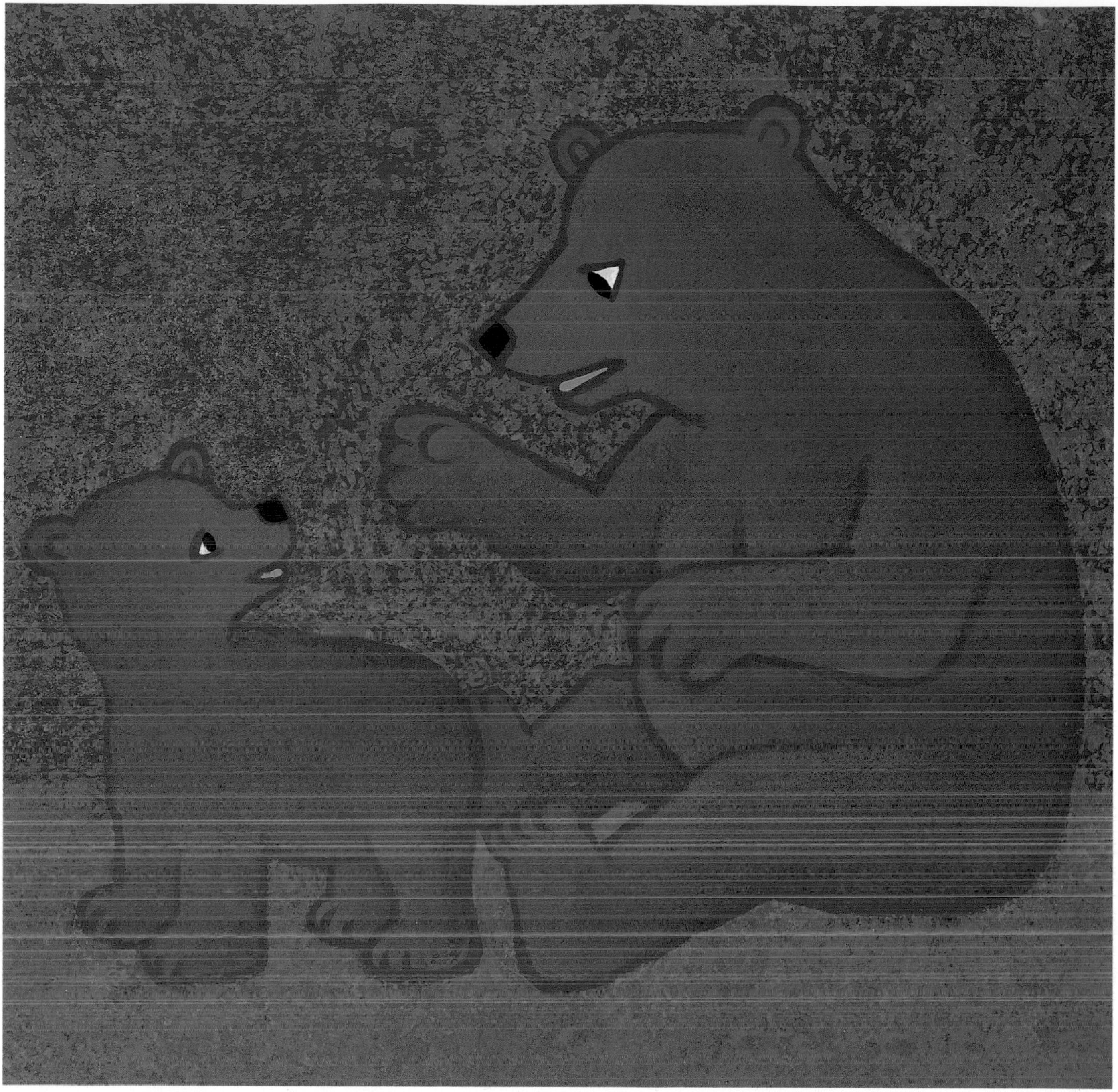

“Okay, Mama,” said Baby Bear. “Just one more thing.”
“What now?” grumbled Mother Bear.

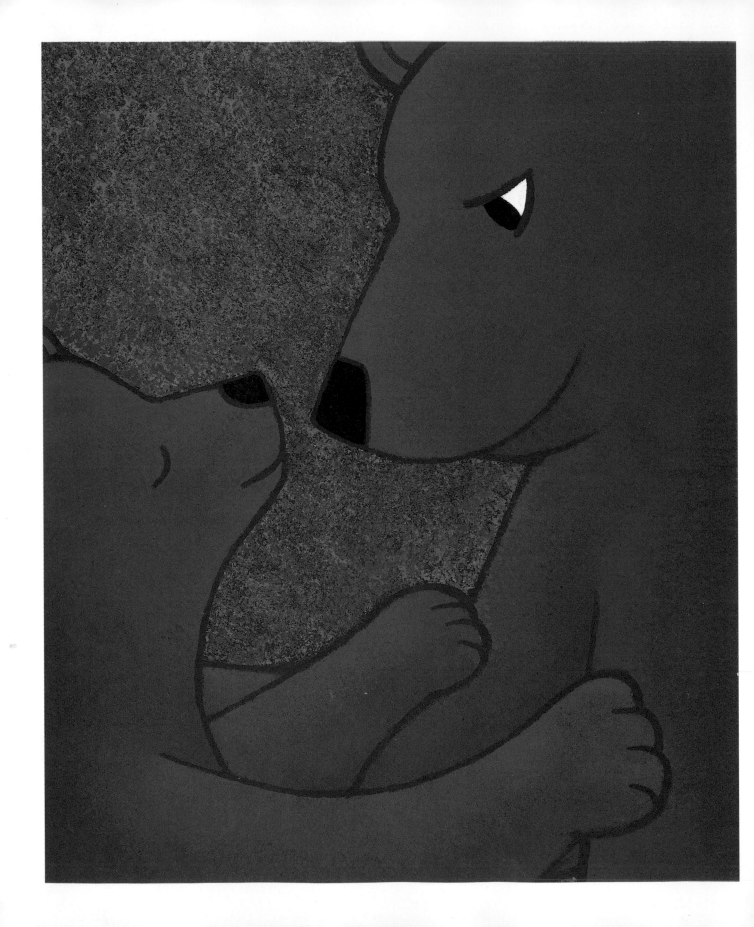

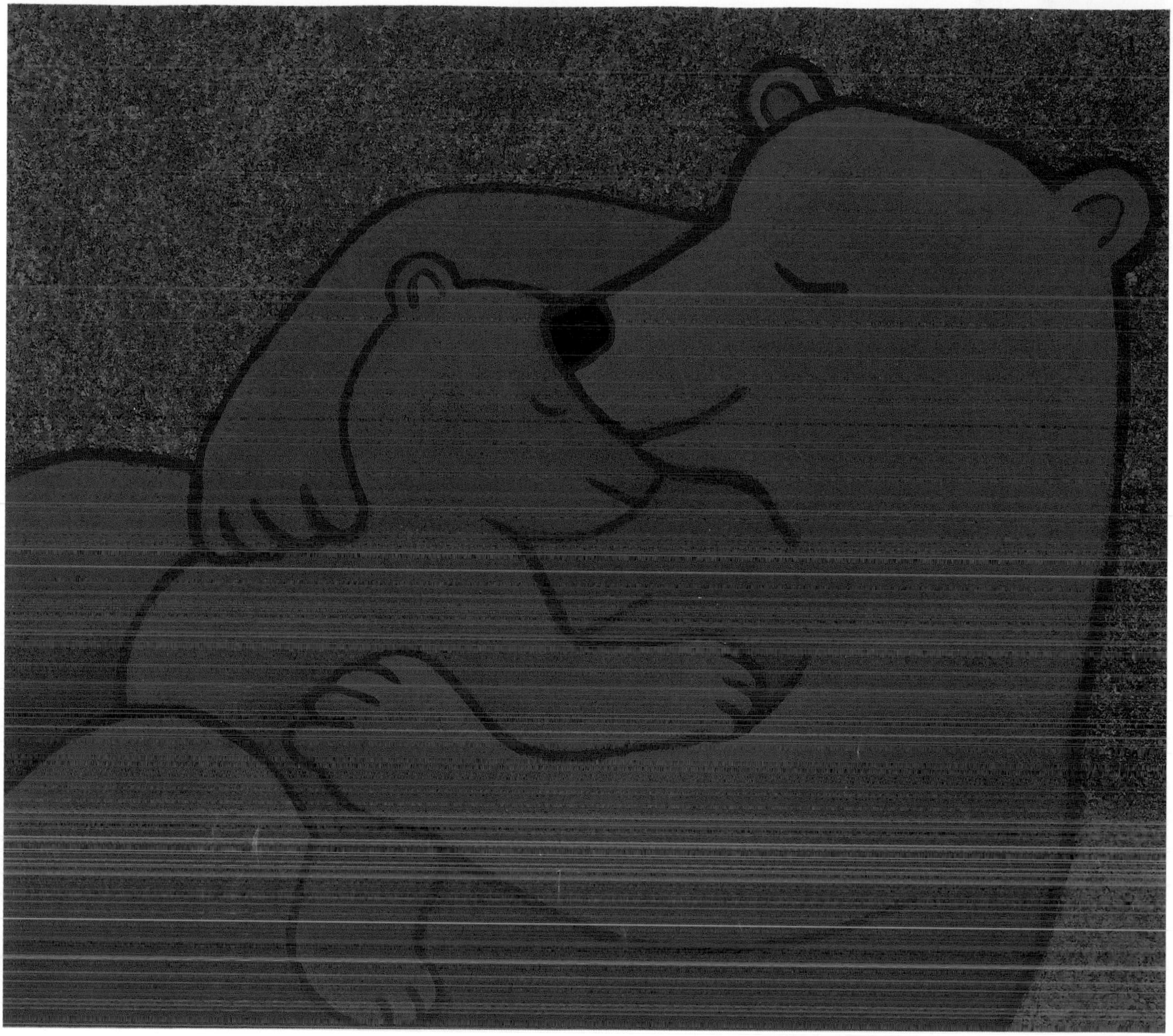

"I want to give you a kiss," said Baby Bear, and he kissed Mother Bear on the nose.

"Good night, Baby Bear," murmured Mother Bear. She drew her cub into a warm embrace and kissed him back.

"Good night, Mama," said Baby Bear, and he closed his eyes. And this time, deep beneath the snow in his cozy, warm cave, Baby Bear fell asleep.